BUILDING A
Model Railroad
Step by Step

David Popp

KALMBACH
BOOKS

625.19
Pop

Printed in the United States of America

11 10 09 08 07   1 2 3 4 5

Visit our Web site at kalmbachbooks.com. Secure online ordering available.

Unless noted, photos were taken by the author.

Publisher's Cataloging-In-Publication Data
(Prepared by The Donohue Group, Inc.)

Popp, David.
  Building a model railroad step by step / David Popp.

   p. : ill. ; cm.

  ISBN: 978-0-89024-689-4

1. Railroads--Models. 2. Railroads--Models--Design and construction. I. Title.

TF197 .P67 2007
625.1/9

About the author

David Popp, a former high school English teacher, is a senior editor for *Model Railroader* magazine. His N scale New Haven layout has been featured regularly in the magazine's "Step by Step" column. In addition to model railroading, David also enjoys historical miniatures war gaming, slot car racing, gardening, and the performing arts. He lives in Waterford, Wis., with his wife, Ingrid, and her grand piano.

Dedication

This book is dedicated to my father and grandfather for the hours we've spent together running trains.

Contents

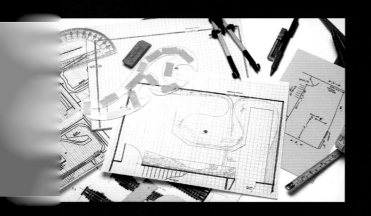

CHAPTER ONE

Getting your layout started

Building your own layout is a fun and rewarding way to enjoy model railroading and share it with others. This New Haven train crosses a bridge over the Naugatuck River on my finished N scale layout.

Want to build a layout? Welcome to one of the most exciting aspects of model railroading! Building a model railroad is a rewarding, fun, and creative project.

Not sure where to start? If you look at building a model railroad as a whole, the project can seem intimidating. However, rest assured that no one builds a layout in one evening, typically not even in 100 evenings. Instead, model railroading is a lifelong hobby. When viewed this way, it's easy to see that a finished layout is actually made up of hundreds of individual projects, completed an hour or two at a time.

Photo **1-1** illustrates my point. I built the red brick factory building in a couple of evenings sitting at the kitchen counter several years ago. The bridge and the stone abutments were another set of two-evening projects. After I'd installed the finished bridge and added it to the layout, it was about a month before I laid the track over it. It was then nearly 12 months before I added the water under it – a project that took an entire week, working 45 minutes a night. In fact, everything you see in the photo was built and added to the layout a little at a time, which brings me to the purpose of this book.

You don't need to know a lot to get started. Much of the model railroading process is really on-the-job training. You'll learn needed skills as you go, and your modeling expertise will grow with each new project. The chapters of this book provide the information you need for each step in the process and include concise projects broken down into bite-size pieces. The examples all take place on my N scale model railroad; however, you can use this information to build a layout of your own design in whatever scale you wish. (More on that later.)

I won't lie to you; model railroading, like anything else, can have moments of frustration. My wife refers to the times I stomp up the stairs after a setback as "those hateful hobby moments." But even frustrations can be great learning experiences. The best advice I can offer when a project isn't going well is to walk away from it for a bit. Go get something to eat or drink, relax a little, then come back and evaluate what's happened. Often, after my emotions have calmed down, I can see where the problem is and correct it before moving on. Taking time to work carefully through a project almost always pays off with success.

So if you like model railroads, but haven't a clue on how to get started, this book is for you. Or if you've been into model railroading for a while, but just haven't gotten around to building a layout yet, this book is also for you. And if you're not sure about the skills, tools, and techniques you need to build your dream layout, this book is definitely for you.

Essential layout-building tools

You may be pleasantly surprised to know that it really doesn't take a whole woodworking shop full of equipment to build a model railroad – even when using the proper tools for each project. Though more-specialized tools can speed up the process considerably, you don't need them if you have the time and patience to work carefully with basic tools.

Throughout the book, sidebars describe some of the basic tools you'll need to complete various projects. Here are a few common-sense tips that will help you get the most out of your layout-building tools:

• Always follow the manufacturer's safety recommendations when operating power tools and use proper eye and ear protection when necessary. Also, take your time when using these tools.

• If purchasing a cordless tool, buy an extra rechargeable battery. Cordless batteries typically recharge quickly, so while you use one battery, you can recharge the other one.

• Cleaning a tool and returning it to its proper place makes it ready to use and easy to find the next time you need it.

• A portable tool cart, caddie, or tackle box works great for collecting and storing the tools you need for a given project.

• Use specialized cutting tools, such as rail and sprue nippers, only for the materials they are designed to cut.

• Taking time to find the right tools can help make the project a success and prolong the life of your tools.

1-2

It's a good idea to know what you want to model before you begin building a layout. Sometimes inspiration for a railroad can be something simple, such as this Micro-Trains N scale boxcar.

PROJECT 1: Choosing a railroad, location, and era

Most modelers can pinpoint the photos, people, events, books, or stories that inspired them to build their model railroads. My N scale Naugatuck Valley RR started with a lone boxcar – a Micro-Trains 40-foot, single-door boxcar decorated in New Haven black and orange, **1-2**. I got the car in December 2001, just a few weeks after I'd come to work for *Model Railroader* magazine. No, that night I didn't drive straight from work to the nearest Home Depot and start buying lumber; it took a bit longer for that to happen. But the boxcar provided the initial push for me to do some research, choose a period and a location, and start scribbling plans.

For you, finding the inspiration to build your model railroad may come from a childhood memory of watching trains in a specific place. In this case, looking at old photos can help fill out your memories, giving you some guidance for modeling your chosen location and railroad. You may have had one or more family members that worked for a particular railroad. If so, you may wish to focus your layout on a specific

road name. Or maybe you simply like how model trains look and find it relaxing to watch them run. If this is you, consider building a layout that will allow you to run trains from different railroads or different eras.

Whatever your choices are for railroad, location, and period, once you've made them, you'll find it much easier to start the next project: choosing a modeling scale.

PROJECT 2: Selecting a scale

Whether you're new to the hobby or have been a modeler for a long time, it's important to choose a scale before beginning your layout. The three most popular model railroad scales are O (1:48 proportion), HO (1:87), and N (1:160), **1-3**.

HO scale is the most common and has the most products available. Trains in this scale feature a good level of detail, and most of the locomotives can accommodate a sound system.

O scale models are about twice as large their HO counterparts. Given their size, O scale trains are fairly heavy, making them impressive models. They often feature a high level of detail, and the locomotives can easily be fitted with a sound system.

Being half the size of HO, N scale models don't typically have the detail found on their larger cousins, and most N scale engines have no space for sound components. However, with N scale, you can get a lot of railroad in a fairly compact space, and this scale is great for running long trains.

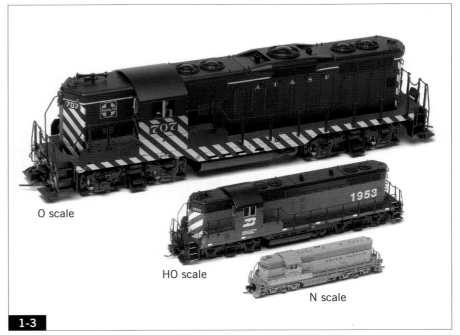

O scale

HO scale

N scale

1-3

These GP9 diesel locomotives show the differences in the three most common scales: O, HO, and N. The manufacturers of these engines are (from largest to smallest) Atlas O, Life-Like Proto 2000, and Atlas. *Jim Forbes*

1-4

Although designing a track plan may seem like a daunting task, breaking it down into several steps makes it easier to execute. *Bill Zuback*

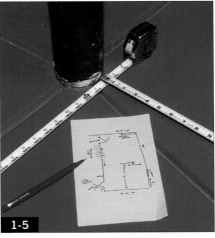

1-5

Determine the position of a pipe or other object by using it as the vertex of a 90-degree angle and measuring it from two walls.

Of all the reasons to choose a scale, the final decision is often directly tied to the amount of space you have to build your railroad. As an example, the plan for my N scale Naugatuck Valley, page 15, fits comfortably in a 13' x 16' room. (This includes a 3-foot aisle around three sides of the layout.) To build the same model railroad in HO scale would require a 23' x 26' room, and for O scale, you'd need a 43' x 46' room.

Changing scales midstream can be costly, so whether your considerations are based on details, sound, train length, or layout space, make sure you choose a scale that is right for you.

PROJECT 3: Drawing your track plan

Before you begin building a model railroad, you need a plan. For some model railroaders, track planning is a hobby all its own – they enjoy figuring out how to capture elements of real railroads and fit them into model form in various size spaces. For me, track planning is simply a means to developing the blueprint for what I want to build.

Although computer programs are available to help plan layouts, you still need to start with some ideas about what you want to build and how much space you have to build it. There is nothing wrong with using good old-fashioned pencil and paper to get the creative juices flowing and start the formative steps that will one day become that high-iron main line through the prairies, mountains, or wherever your trains are going to run.

STEP 1 Claiming territory

Before cutting the line through that mountain pass or bridging that river valley, you need to have a place to put it all. More importantly, you need to know just how big the place is and identify obstacles that require special attention when designing your layout.

Taking accurate measurements of the railroad room is a must before

1-6

Drawing a layout on graph paper having ¼" squares makes it easy for figuring smaller measurements. *Bill Zuback*

1-7

Doodling is helpful in exploring possible track schematics and layout shapes. *Bill Zuback*

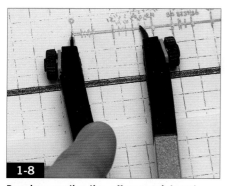

1-8

Drawing a radius line offers a quick and accurate radius measurement when drawing curves. *Bill Zuback*

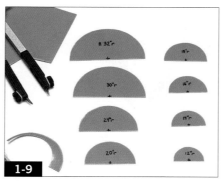

1-9

Common curve sizes for N gauge templates range from 12" to 32". *Bill Zuback*

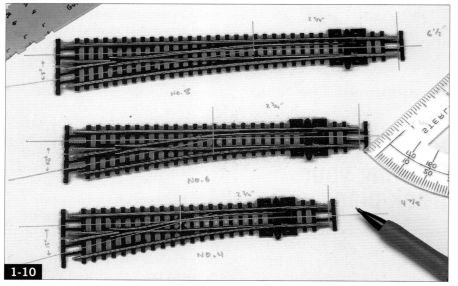

1-10

Marking dimensions on a turnout measuring guide provides a handy reference for drawing turnouts. *Bill Zuback*

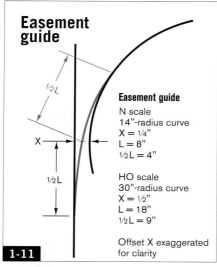

1-11

Illustration by Kellie Jaeger

Easement guide

½ L

X

½ L

Easement guide

N scale
14"-radius curve
X = ¼"
L = 8"
½L = 4"

HO scale
30"-radius curve
X = ½"
L = 18"
½L = 9"

Offset X exaggerated for clarity

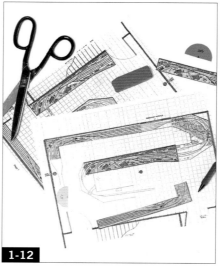

1-12

Carrying features from the first draft of a plan to final design is often done simply by cutting and pasting. *Bill Zuback*

doing any other planning. Windows, heat vents, plumbing, furnace access, and support columns all need to be accurately recorded in your room plan. Also, keep in mind that doors opening into a room will need to have clearance.

Begin with a rough sketch of the space. As you work your way around the room with a tape measure, fill in the dimensions for walls, doors, windows, and other features. If you are in a basement or attic, you will also need to mark any pipes or support columns on your drawing. To establish the position of pipes or columns in the middle of a room, use the object as the vertex of a 90-degree angle and measure its distance from two walls, **1-5**.

Another feature to keep in mind is head room. If you are in a space that has low hanging objects, mark those on the plan as well.

STEP 2 Choosing an illustration scale

Now that you have all your room measurements written down, you need to select a scale for your room and track plan drawing. I like to work in ½" = 1' scale. This scale accommodates a fairly accurate rendition of trackwork and scenery, and except for very large room plans, it fits easily on a photocopier.

Using the dimensions you've recorded, draw your layout room on a sheet of graph paper with ¼" squares, **1-6**. In ½" scale, each ¼" square equals 6", which makes figuring smaller measurements a little easier. When the drawing is finished, make photocopies of it so that you can quickly sketch new drafts as your ideas develop.

STEP 3 Doodling

Before investing time and effort into making the perfect track plan on the first try, it's important to explore potential track schematics and layout shapes in your space. For the doodling stage, I took my room plan, reduced it 50 percent on a photocopier, and reproduced four per page. Then I experimented with various ways to fit the desired features into the space.

In this plan, I wanted a mainline railroad with a branch line. I attempted to work these two features in each doodle, **1-7**, while maintaining an open path to and from my workshop. Once you come up with an idea you like, try drawing the plan in ½" scale.

STEP 4 Making curve templates

You can draw layout plans faster with a few helpful tools. A compass works well when drawing curves. By making a radius line, **1-8**, you can set your compass to the correct radius and transfer the markings to the plan.

A speedy alternative is making cardboard or styrene templates of common curve sizes, **1-9**. After drawing each radius on a sheet of gray styrene with a compass, I cut them out with a pair of scissors. Make sure to label the size of each template with permanent marker.

STEP 5 Drawing accurate turnouts

Leaving adequate space for turnouts is a common problem when drawing track plans. A simple solution to drawing correctly sized turnouts on your plan is to purchase a few samples and make a measuring guide. I constructed my N scale turnout guide using one of each size of Peco's N scale code 55 turnouts. After photocopying the turnouts, I used the guide to measure the length of each one and find its angle of divergence, marking the dimensions on the guide for easy reference.

As with the curves, you can also make a template to help maintain correct turnout lengths on your track plan. I drew mine on a sheet of paper first and then cut the template to match. When cutting the correct angle, you will need to extend the line for the diverging route well beyond the turnout because a template for ½" scale turnouts is fairly small.

STEP 6 Drawing easements

On real railroads, straight (tangent) track connects to curves with a gradual transition called an easement. An easement is a curve of decreasing radius that helps ease a train into the arc of the circular curve. Including easements on a model railroad makes trackwork look more realistic and helps the trains operate better. From a design aspect, easements allow you to use slightly

Naugatuck RR history

Kent W. Cochrane

The real Naugatuck Branch got its start in 1849. Chartered as the Naugatuck RR (nicknamed the Naugy) in Waterbury, Conn., the main line ran from Winsted south to Devon, Conn., and was completed in little more than a year. Waterbury, shown in the photo, was the hub of the New Haven's Naugatuck Branch. At Devon, the Naugatuck connected with the New York & New Haven RR and had an agreement with that line to run Naugatuck RR trains all the way to Bridgeport, Conn. There, the Naugatuck used steamships to transfer passengers and freight to New York City until the NY&NH completed its line to New York a few years later.

Though the Naugatuck suffered some initial growing pains, largely because of periodic flooding of the Naugatuck River, the line prospered in the growing Connecticut industrial river valley. Additional improvements during these early years included opening a branch line to Watertown, Conn., west of Waterbury; making the main line and its bridges more flood-resistant; constructing railroad shops and docks at Bridgeport; and double-tracking the southern half of the railroad.

Despite the Naugy's prosperity through the Civil War and beyond, increasing competitive pressure from the New York, New Haven & Hartford RR (formerly the NY&NH) resulted in financial woes for the line in the 1880s. As a result, the Naugy leased its property to the NH in 1887. This was meant to be a 99-year lease, but the line was deeded over to the NH in the early 1900s. The New Haven ran the Naugatuck Branch until the railroad was absorbed into the Penn Central on January 1, 1969.

tighter radius curves, as easements make turns seem bigger than they really are.

Because of the scale at which you're drawing track plans, easements will barely show. The guide, **1-11**, gives the two most basic measurements for figuring an easement: X = the offset measurement and ½L = the length of the easement from where the curve and the straight track meet. Since the X measurement for N scale is ¼" and in HO it's ½", drawing an easement is simple – just offset the curve from your straight track by a pencil-lead width and continue drawing. The ½L measurement is more important to remember – you can't place a straight turnout in that length because it will be built with a curve.

STEP 7 Drawing to your heart's content

Perhaps the most important lesson in track planning is do not be afraid to start over. Often, I wind up with a few features in a first draft that seem to work well, so I will photocopy them, cut them out, and try working them into a new plan, **1-12**.

Building a model railroad from plans that reflect your specific modeling interests is a very rewarding experience. You should now have enough information to get a good start. For a much more detailed look at track planning, pick up a copy of John Armstrong's book *Track Planning for Realistic Operation* (Kalmbach).

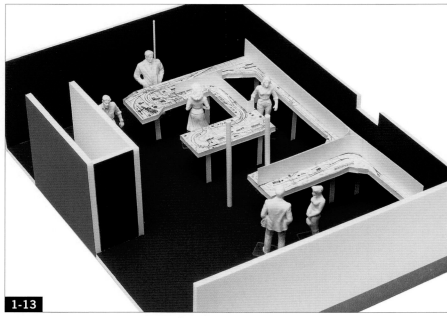

1-13

This 3-D model shows that, if expanded, my Naugatuck Valley layout could support operations for six people and still have room to grow. *Jim Forbes*

PROJECT 4: Modeling your layout in 3-D

As an optional step in your layout-planning process, it may be a good idea to do a test-fit. Using a technique I picked up from my brother, an architectural illustrator, I built a 3-D model of the layout and the room, **1-13**.

Building a 3-D layout model is an easy one- or two-evening project,

and the finished result brings to light design and construction considerations that don't show up on a paper-and-pencil track plan – considerations that are much easier to fix if you haven't actually built them yet!

STEP 1 Preparing the track plan

A 3-D layout model is handy to take to your friends' houses or club meetings for design input, so you don't want it to be so big that you can't use it. For this reason, I built mine in ½" scale – my finished model is roughly 12" x 16", making it simple to transport.

Since you've already drawn your track plan, this a quick-and-easy project. You'll need to cut up the plan to make the model, so make a photocopy of it. Also, if you've drawn your track plan in a scale larger than ½", you can have it reduced at a copy shop.

You can give your track plan more definition by using colored pencils or markers to fill in features such as water, roads, tree lines, and fields, **1-14**. Then mount the plan on a piece of foam-core, craft construction board using a quick-drying adhesive, such as a glue stick. Next, cut the track plan from the foam core using a sharp hobby knife and a metal straightedge, **1-15**.

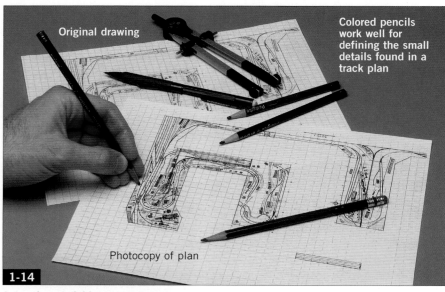

Original drawing

Colored pencils work well for defining the small details found in a track plan

Photocopy of plan

1-14

Color gives definition to the features on a track plan. *Jim Forbes*

STEP 2 Adding legs and backdrops

The next step is adding the layout's support structure and backdrops. You can make a network of legs and braces from strips of scrap foam core, **1-16**. To get the proper 3-D effect, you need to make sure that the layout's base height is correct, taking into account the thickness of the foam core (⁷⁄₃₂") on which the track plan is mounted. My layout's base height is 42" (in ½" scale my model layout is 1¾" tall), so the foam-core legs are 1¹⁷⁄₃₂" tall.

This is also a good time to add any backdrops, especially if you're using them as scene dividers as I have. Backdrops are an important detail to include since they will give the proper sight lines when the 3-D model is viewed from eye-level.

Because backdrops are often curved, thin cardboard is a good material to use here. To form smooth curves in the backdrop, try wrapping the cardboard around a tube or rod, such as the hobby-knife handle, **1-17**. Once the curve is formed, cement the backdrop to the track plan using white glue. Cementing two pieces of cardboard back-to-back gives you a rigid scene divider.

STEP 3 Building your room

When the model layout is finished, it's time to build the layout room. You'll need dimensions of your room to build this part of the model. Build the room in a contrasting color of foam core so the layout model is easier to view.

Following the room's dimensions, start by cutting out the floor. Cut the walls next and include any windows or doors. Also, be sure to take into account the ⁷⁄₃₂" thickness of the foam-core floor when measuring the model's wall height. My basement walls are 96" tall; in ½" scale that's 4". I added the thickness of the floor to that dimension, making my model's walls 4⁷⁄₃₂" tall.

Cement the walls to the floor with white glue and reinforce the joint with 2" masking tape, **1-18**. Since the room model can be used over and over until you've established your layout's design, reinforcing the corners with tape is a good idea.

At this point, you should add any obstructions in the room. For me, they

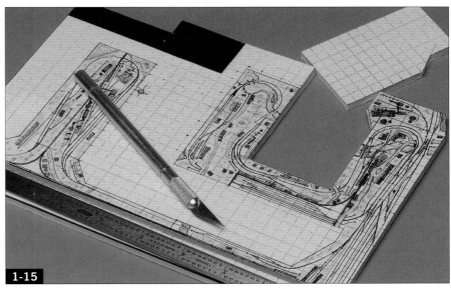

1-15

A hobby knife with a sharp blade and a straightedge should be used to cut out a plan cemented to foam core. *Jim Forbes*

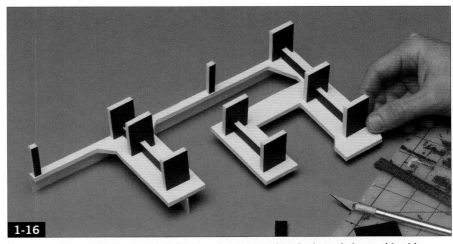

1-16

Foam-core legs cut to the proper height can be cemented to the layout's base with white glue. *Jim Forbes*

included a stairwell, water-service pipe, support post, and soil stack, **1-19**. I made the pipes and the post from ¹⁄₁₆" and ³⁄₁₆" white Plastruct rods. I built the stairwell from foam core but made it removable in order to get a better operator's-eye view of the model.

STEP 4 Adding the human element

Now comes the fun part – putting it all together. With the room complete, you can add the layout model, positioning it to get the best fit if your plan allows for some wiggle room.

The next step is adding a human element to your model by placing some scale figures in the room. You can make simple figures by sketching stick people

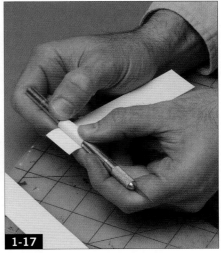

1-17

Wrap cardboard around a hobby knife handle to form smooth curves in a backdrop. *Jim Forbes*

Make sure the walls meet the floor at a 90-degree angle before gluing. Use masking tape to reinforce the wall-to-floor joint. *Jim Forbes*

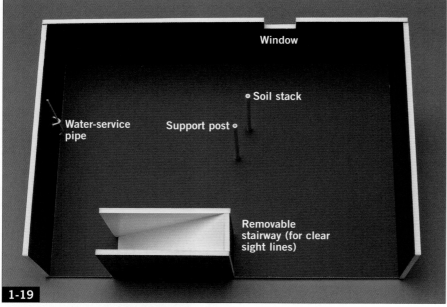

Window

Soil stack

Water-service pipe

Support post

Removable stairway (for clear sight lines)

1-19

Add obstructions, doors, windows, and stairs to your room model. *Jim Forbes*

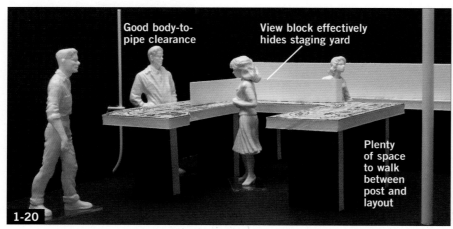

Good body-to-pipe clearance

View block effectively hides staging yard

Plenty of space to walk between post and layout

1-20

Placing figures in the model helps determine any spacing problems with obstructions or aisles. *Jim Forbes*

or using photos of people approximately 2½" to 3" tall (5½' to 6' in ½" scale). Cement the images to some foam-core scraps, cut them out, and stand them up in the 3-D model.

As an alternative, you can do what I did and purchase a package of no. 57820 unpainted 1:24 proportion (½" scale) Preiser figures. The figures come with clear plastic bases, so you can position them around the model at will.

Adding figures to your 3-D model lets you see what the layout room will look like full of operators, giving you a realistic idea of how comfortable or crowded the aisles will be, **1-20**. Figures also help determine clearance trouble points for people between the layout and objects in the room.

This is really just the beginning of what you can do with a layout model. Once you've settled on a track plan and are happy with how the layout will fit in your room, you can take the project a step further by adding modeling-clay scenery contours. You can also make structures from stripwood or styrene and add them to the model.

Five track planning tips

1. Making templates for common items such as the room, curves, and turnouts speeds up the design process.

2. When drawing a door that swings into the train room, draw its opening arc to show the space it requires.

3. Drawing turnouts accurately is important for a successful layout design.

4. Easements help trains run smoother, and a sharper curve with an easement looks better than a broader curve without one.

5. Photocopying the elements you like from previous plans saves redrawing time.

Track plan for the Naugatuck Valley

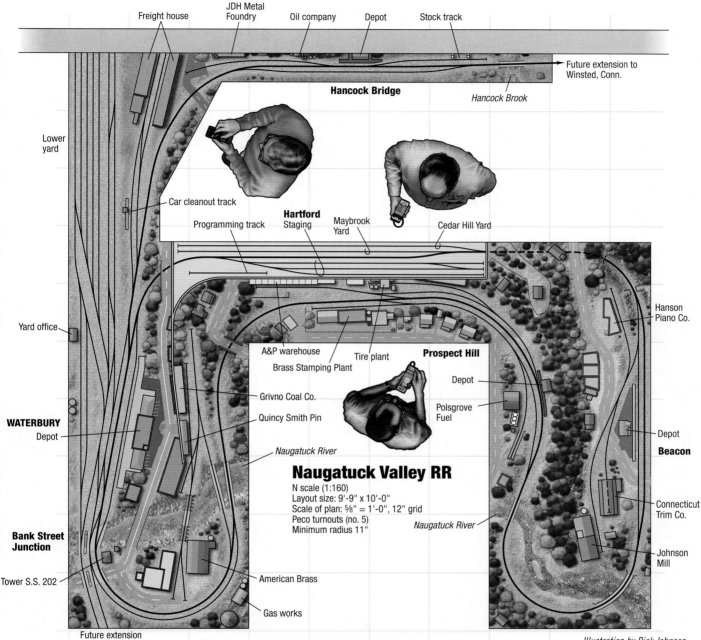

Freight house
JDH Metal Foundry
Oil company
Depot
Stock track
Future extension to Winsted, Conn.

Hancock Bridge
Hancock Brook

Lower yard

Car cleanout track

Hartford
Staging

Programming track

Maybrook Yard

Cedar Hill Yard

Yard office

Hanson Piano Co.

A&P warehouse
Tire plant
Prospect Hill
Brass Stamping Plant

Depot

Grivno Coal Co.

Polsgrove Fuel

Quincy Smith Pin

WATERBURY
Depot

Naugatuck River

Naugatuck Valley RR
N scale (1:160)
Layout size: 9'-9" x 10'-0"
Scale of plan: ⅝" = 1'-0", 12" grid
Peco turnouts (no. 5)
Minimum radius 11"

Naugatuck River

Depot

Beacon

Connecticut Trim Co.

Bank Street Junction

American Brass

Johnson Mill

Tower S.S. 202

Gas works

Future extension

Illustration by Rick Johnson

The layout featured in this book is my own N scale model railroad, the Naugatuck Valley. It's based on a branch line of the New York, New Haven & Hartford RR (called the New Haven) and is set in the fall of 1959. The line follows the Naugatuck River Valley and serves the towns and industries along its banks. My track plan centers on the line's hub at Waterbury, Conn., and includes pieces of the radiating lines running north to Winsted, Conn., south to Derby Junction (connecting to the New Haven's yards at Cedar Hill, Conn., and Maybrook, N.Y.), and east to Hartford.

I designed the layout to be built in stages. The first part, including the towns of Beacon and Prospect Hill, was started in my apartment several years ago. After my wife and I bought our home, I added the Waterbury and Hancock Bridge section. Now that those are finished, my next step is building the northern portion, including the terminus at Winsted. At some point, I also plan to add the rest of the industries at Waterbury, extending from the southern end of the layout.

Building a model railroad in stages has some distinct benefits. By finishing only a portion of

the layout at a time, you'll find you have a nice variety of smaller-sized projects to complete before beginning the next section. And, when you start that next section, you'll have acquired more skills, making the work easier and more enjoyable. Perhaps the biggest advantage of building a layout in stages, however, is the feeling of accomplishment — you now have a finished scene or two to share with visitors. And don't forget it also means you can run some trains, which is what keeps the hobby fun and exciting.

2-1

CHAPTER TWO

Building benchwork and adding backdrops

Building model railroad benchwork is easier than you might think. With just basic carpentry skills and a few common tools, you can build all the benchwork your layout will need, one portable section at a time.

A great model railroad starts with solid benchwork. Much has been written on the subject, and you can build benchwork from a variety of materials including wood, steel, plastic, and foam board. In the end, it seems there's almost as much variety in benchwork construction as there are model railroads.

However, if you're a person that moves often (like me), you'll want to consider building your model railroad so it can move with you. I've taken down more than my fair share of layouts due to moves, and it's a frustrating experience to have to start over from scratch each time. With that in mind, we'll look at a simple method for building benchwork in freestanding sections. These can be combined to build a variety of model railroad designs yet can be made portable enough to move without much effort, **2-1**.

Along the way, we'll also look at using foam insulation board as a base scenery layer as well as explore how to make easy-to-use backdrops from sheet styrene.

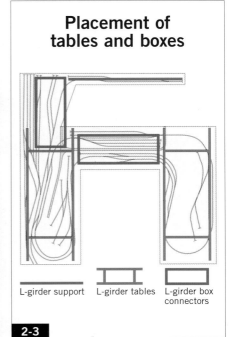

Placement of tables and boxes

L-girder support   L-girder tables   L-girder box connectors

2-3

Illustration by Jay Smith

2-2

Moving and expanding a layout is easy to do when it is supported by a benchwork system of tables and boxes.

PROJECT 1: Creating easy, versatile benchwork

When I set out to build my N scale Naugatuck Valley RR, it was to be a simple project layout for the magazine, built in my apartment while I waited for our house to be constructed. (For the story of its origin and track plan, see the January 2003 *Model Railroader*.) Because we were getting ready to move, I made the layout portable, building it on a 32"-wide hollow-core door and supporting the entire affair with an inexpensive folding table. (The 18" x 48" extension had its own support leg.)

True to its portable design, the little model railroad followed obediently to my new, empty basement. When I decided to expand the layout, **2-2**, I knew I'd have to raise the height and mount the layout on more substantial benchwork – the folding table had to go!

The benchwork can be completed in four simple steps, starting with making tables and boxes.

STEP 1 Making tables and boxes

There are a number of ways to build benchwork for a model railroad, and books such as Jeff Wilson's *Basic Model Railroad Benchwork* are a great source for getting started.

I used a variation on the L-girder theme, developed by former *Model Railroader* editor Linn Westcott in the 1960s. An L girder is made from two pieces of lumber, usually a 1 x 2 flange glued and screwed on top of a 1 x 3 or 1 x 4, forming an L-shaped beam. This easy-to-build structural member supports a great deal of weight and is useful in a variety of benchwork designs. It uses less lumber yet is strong and provides a number of options for joining other boards to it.

Since I was using hollow-core doors for the main portions of the layout, I chose to build a system of supporting tables and connecting boxes using L-girder beams, **2-3**.

The tables are freestanding and include a storage shelf. These benchwork sections support the hollow-core door components of the layout and use the 1 x 2 L-girder flange as a screw cleat.

The connecting boxes are also made with L girders. These support

the framed layout sections that join the hollow-core doors. The boxes are bolted to the support tables with ¼" carriage bolts and wing nuts, so if need be, the layout benchwork can be quickly disassembled and put back together.

The combination of support tables and connecting boxes form a solid benchwork system, with the versatility of easily adding new sections to the existing layout.

STEP 2 Constructing tables

The benchwork support tables are made from 1 x 2 and 1 x 3 clear (knot-free) pine lumber. Though clear pine is more expensive, it's a high-quality construction material, making it easier to build straight, level benchwork. The dimensions I used support 32"-36" hollow-core interior doors, **2-4**, but you can change the measurements to accommodate any type or size layout.

I did all the construction in sub-assemblies, and most of the fabricated parts are glued and screwed together. Be sure to drill pilot holes for all screws to avoid splitting the wood. The legs, L-girder frame, shelf, and braces are attached to each other using ¼" carriage bolts with washers and wing nuts.

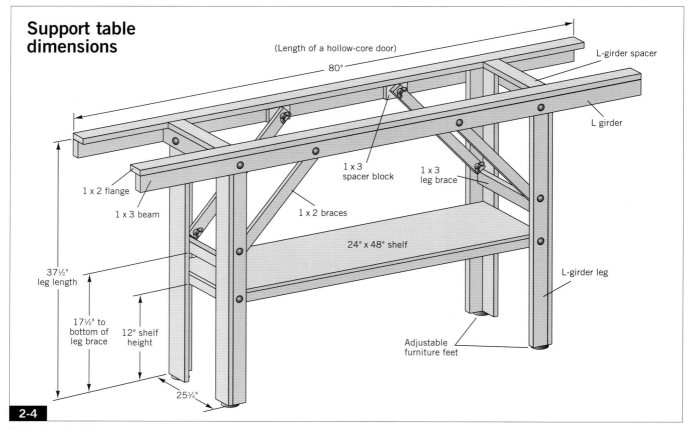

Support table dimensions

(Length of a hollow-core door)

80"

L-girder spacer

L girder

1 x 2 flange

1 x 3 beam

1 x 3 spacer block

1 x 3 leg brace

1 x 2 braces

24" x 48" shelf

37½" leg length

L-girder leg

17½" to bottom of leg brace

12" shelf height

Adjustable furniture feet

25¾"

2-4

Illustration by Jay Smith

2-5

After checking that things are square, use bar clamps to hold the table frame during final assembly.

2-6

Glue and screw leg joints together as in L-girder construction.

2-7

Use a 1 x 3 spacer block to provide a flush fit between the leg brace and L girder.

2-8

Install adjustable furniture feet in the legs to level the table.

2-9

Brace the table with a framed shelf that can be used for storage.

Connecting box

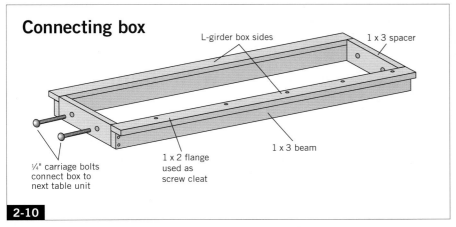

L-girder box sides

1 x 3 spacer

¼" carriage bolts connect box to next table unit

1 x 2 flange used as screw cleat

1 x 3 beam

2-10

Illustration by Jay Smith

L girders are made using 1 x 2s for the flange and 1 x 3s for the beam, **2-5**. If you're building spans longer than 8 feet, you'll want to use 1 x 4s or larger for the beams.

The legs are built similarly to L girders, except that the 1 x 3 sits on the top edge of the 1 x 2, **2-6**. My layout's legs are 37½" high (giving me a layout track height of 42"), but you may want them taller, depending on how high you want your layout. Each pair of legs is joined by a 1 x 3 brace.

The leg braces are made from 1 x 2s and bolted to the table assembly with ¼" carriage bolts. The 1 x 3 spacer block allows a flush fit between the leg brace and the L girder, **2-7**.

Adjustable furniture feet, found in most hardware stores, come with a friction-fit nylon socket and a threaded foot, **2-8**. Drill the appropriate size hole, tap in the socket using a hammer, and screw in the foot.

Each table has its own storage shelf, used to brace the legs, **2-9**. The shelf is made with a 1 x 2 frame covered with a ¼" lauan plywood top. You could easily enclose the shelf with removable panels to hide its contents.

STEP 3 Connecting boxes

Though hollow-core doors are easy to work with, their rectangular shape and size are somewhat limiting. Because of this, I used doors for only the main portions of the layout. For the in-between parts, I built simple connector sections from 1 x 2s, covering them with a ¼" plywood top.

To support these sections, I built L-girder boxes, **2-10**. The boxes bolt onto the table units with ¼" carriage bolts; they support the connecting layout sections and firm up the entire benchwork structure, **2-11**.

For extensions from the layout that don't connect to another table, you can add one or more leg assemblies (like those used for the table supports). I used this technique to support the long tail section, **2-3**. This tail section will eventually be tied into another support table.

STEP 4 Attaching layout sections

Once the benchwork is assembled and leveled, you can attach the layout to it. For the framed layout sections, simply run screws through the L-girder flanges into the frame, **2-12**.

Working with hollow-core doors is a bit trickier. These have a solid wood frame, approximately 1" wide, that runs around the perimeter of the door. The center, as the name implies, is hollow, usually containing a web of cardboard spacers to support the thin plywood exterior. Therefore, you really can't run screws into the center of the door and expect them to hold well.

For the hollow-core door layout sections, I ran screws through the flanges near the ends, sinking them into the door's frame. I then carefully set several more screws through the thin center of the door just to tack it in place. With that, your layout should now be firmly supported.

2-11

Connector boxes can be used to span the area between layout tables.

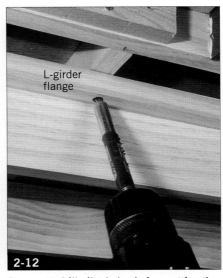

L-girder flange

2-12

Be sure to drill pilot holes before setting the screws.

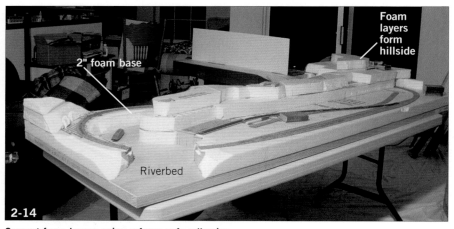

2-13

Extruded polystyrene insulation board provides a solid base for scenery construction.

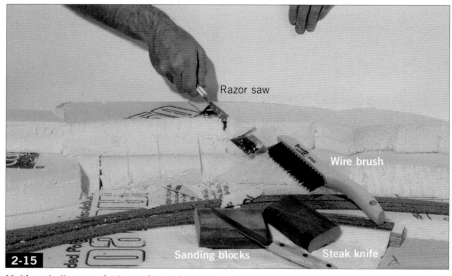

2" foam base

Foam layers form hillside

Riverbed

2-14

Cement foam layers using a foam-safe adhesive.

Razor saw

Wire brush

Sanding blocks

Steak knife

2-15

Making shallow, vertical cuts in the foam enables you to shape the material more easily by allowing you to work on small sections at a time.

PROJECT 2:
Landscaping with foam

With the benchwork built, it's time to add the initial layer of scenery. A number of years ago, I learned that extruded polystyrene insulation board makes a great starting point for many scenery projects. This useful building material comes in an assortment of sizes and colors and is available at most lumberyards and home centers. Foam board is lightweight yet reasonably strong and can be cut, filed, drilled, sanded, rasped, glued, and painted. It holds its shape well and is not affected by moisture. It also has the advantage of allowing a modeler to easily plant trees and other scenery features just by poking holes into the foam.

STEP 1 Layering foam

There are many ways in which you can use foam insulation board to form a scenery base. My favorite is the topographic method – I build up hillsides, riverbanks, and even the track right-of-way by gluing layers of foam board in place. The unsculpted layers of foam look a lot like the contour lines of a topographic map, **2-14**.

To make straight (and gently curved) cuts in the foam, you can use the score-and-snap method commonly associated with styrene. After marking the cut line with a marker, cut about halfway through the board with a sharp utility knife. Next, bend the foam along the incision until the piece snaps free. For tighter curved cuts, I use a razor saw with a fine blade (42 teeth per inch), although I've also occasionally used a common steak knife. Keep in mind, however, that the more coarse the cutting instrument, the more foam dust you'll have to clean up. As a result, it's a good idea to wear a disposable filter mask when sawing or sanding this material.

I started constructing my layout's scenery by gluing a base layer of 2" foam to the benchwork with Liquid Nails latex adhesive. (I've also used latex caulk with good results.) When working with foam insulation board, make sure you use a foam-safe adhesive. Solvent-based adhesives will eat into the foam instead of cementing it in place.

With the base layer of foam in place, I then drew the track plan on its surface and installed cork roadbed for the track. I used Midwest N scale roadbed, cementing it to the foam with yellow carpenter's glue and tacking it in place with T pins until the glue dried.

Next, I added the foam hillside that runs through the layout's center. I built this up by cementing two additional layers of 2" foam on top of the base layer, pinning the layers in place until the adhesive set.

STEP 2 Roughing in the shape

Let the adhesive dry thoroughly before starting to shape the foam. Because it's an insulation material, foam resists airflow. Therefore, it can take the adhesive a lot longer to dry than the suggested time. I gave my hillside a full week to dry before starting on the next step.

You can use many different tools to shape foam, including hot-wire foam cutters, rasps, wire brushes, and various knives. One of my favorite foam-shaping tools, however, is my trusty razor saw.

To shape above-grade features like my hillside, I started by cutting shallow vertical grooves in the stacked foam layers at 2" intervals, **2-15**. These cuts allowed me to work on small sections of hill at a time – this is especially helpful when making concave cuts with the razor saw. After removing the initial pieces to establish the slope, I made successively shallower cuts with the saw to round the top.

Cut away too much foam? No problem, just cement the piece back on and start over! Foam is very forgiving.

Making below-grade features that don't go all the way down to the benchwork, such as fills, creek beds, and small valleys, is a two-part process. First, I made the angle cut from the top that defines the slope of the lower area to be removed, **2-16**. When making these cuts, I work the thin razor saw blade into the foam using short, gentle strokes. Next, I made the outside

Construction hand tools

A set of basic hand tools is a must for any construction project, and I selected these for their fundamental usefulness. The hammer, tape measure, level, utility knife, and screwdrivers (one flat-head and one Phillips) are all common tools. I chose the small square (called a speed square) for its compact size and built-in angle guide, both of which are helpful when marking cut lines.

There are two types of clamps: bar clamps and spring clamps, which are almost like having a spare set of hands. Bar clamps can hold larger items, and the spring clamps are great for working in tight places.

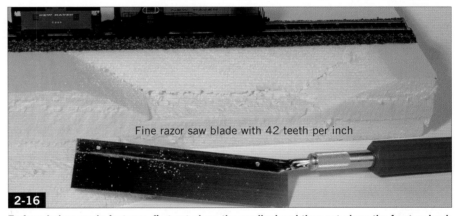

Fine razor saw blade with 42 teeth per inch

2-16

To form below-grade features, first cut along the roadbed and then cut along the front or back edge.

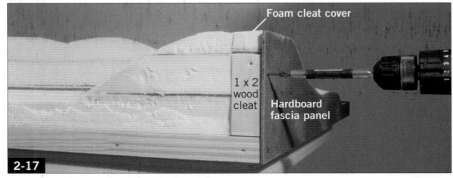

Foam cleat cover

1 x 2 wood cleat

Hardboard fascia panel

2-17

Before screwing the fascia boards in place, drill screw holes in the cleats to avoid splitting the wood.

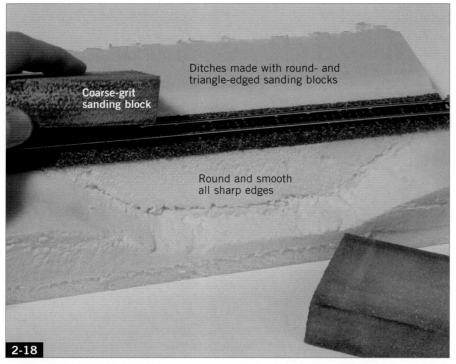

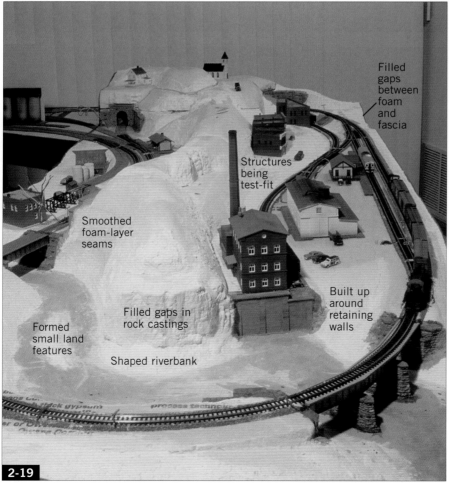

Coarse-grit sanding block

Ditches made with round- and triangle-edged sanding blocks

Round and smooth all sharp edges

2-18

Sanding blocks can create landscape features as well as provide a smooth, finished shape.

Filled gaps between foam and fascia

Structures being test-fit

Smoothed foam-layer seams

Built up around retaining walls

Formed small land features

Filled gaps in rock castings

Shaped riverbank

2-19

Sculptamold is good for filling gaps and making smooth transitions between foam layers.

cut from the fascia edge or the backdrop edge.

To form larger below-grade areas, I removed whole sections of the 2" base foam layer down to the benchwork and then filled the space with a layer of thinner foam.

STEP 3 Adding fascia

With the rough shape of the layout defined, I added the hardboard fascia. If you don't need to remove the fascia, you can cement it straight to the foam with construction adhesive. However, since I needed access to wiring for the Digital Command Control (DCC) system that I ran through the foam, I made my fascia panels removable, 2-17.

As the foam is not dense enough to hold screws securely, I added wood cleats to the corners and at intervals along the edge of the layout. I made the cleats from 1 x 2 blocks of pine, cutting them ½" shorter than the height of the foam at each cleat location.

I embedded the blocks in the layout by cutting away a cleat-size section of the foam with my razor saw and then cementing the block in place with construction adhesive. Finally, to hide the block completely, I made a foam cleat cover by cutting off the top ½" of the removed section of foam and cementing it to the top of the block.

STEP 4 Finishing the shape

Once you've established the landscape's rough shape, you can give it a more-natural look by sanding the foam. I used an assortment of coarse- and medium-grit sponge-rubber sanding blocks, 2-18. The blocks are inexpensive, available with differently shaped edges, and well suited for finishing the foam-sculpting process.

I started with a coarse-grit block with a round edge to sand into the inside corners and removed the pointed angles made by cutting the fills and riverbanks. Next, I used a wedge-shaped block to dig deeper land features into the foam, such as erosion marks in the hillside and ditches along the railroad right-of-way. I then used a medium-grit square block to sand all sharp edges and smooth the rough spots left behind by the saw. I also sanded the layout edges to match the contours of the layout fascia.

When sawing and sanding the foam, it's a good idea to have your shop vacuum handy. Foam dust is attracted by static electricity, and if you're not careful, before long, you, your tools, and the work surface wind up covered in the stuff. Stopping periodically to vacuum the work area (and yourself) is a good idea and helps keep the layout room and the rest of the house neat.

STEP 5 Filling the gaps

After the shaping was finished, I installed the rock castings, abutments, bridge piers, styrene roads, and retaining walls. (See chapter 4 for most of these details.) I cemented all these items to the foam with latex caulk. I then filled gaps, gouges, and remaining sharp inside-angle cuts in the foam and formed the riverbank with Sculptamold, **2-19**.

Sculptamold is a lightweight paper and plaster product that is much easier and neater to work with than ordinary plaster. It's available at hobby shops and craft stores in 3-, 25-, and 50-pound bags. Though Sculptamold dries hard in approximately 24 hours, it's a good idea to apply it in small batches as it sets in about 10 minutes.

For my layout, I worked with one cup of Sculptamold at a time, mixing it with water in a plastic bowl (a large cottage-cheese container works well) until the material had the consistency of thick mashed potatoes. I then applied it to the layout with a putty knife or worked it into place with my fingers as necessary. If you get Sculptamold where you don't want it, clean it off with a wet paper towel before it dries – it'll be a lot harder to remove later!

In addition to smoothing out the landscape, I also used Sculptamold to fill the gaps between the foam and the fascia. To keep the material from sticking to the fascia boards, I slipped pieces of wax paper between the fascia and the foam layer.

Once the Sculptamold had dried, the layout was ready for trackwork and its basic scenery layer.

2-20

Even a simple backdrop of sky and clouds adds depth and detail to a layout.

PROJECT 3: Making styrene backdrops and painting clouds

Imagine one morning you looked out your front window and, across the street above the tree line beyond your neighbor's house, all you could see was a concrete wall; or worse yet, suppose a workbench filled your view! Not a very pretty picture, is it?

Nothing gives a model railroad a more finished look than a backdrop, **2-20**. Whether the backdrop is highly detailed, featuring rolling hills and distant mountain scenery, or like mine, a simple blue sky with some wispy clouds, a backdrop helps preserve the illusion that the model world extends beyond what you see on the layout.

I've built nearly 20 layouts, but it wasn't until the last four or five that I really discovered the value of including a backdrop in the initial construction phase. Until that point I'd considered backdrops as an afterthought or a luxury item – they cost time and materials better spent on the models. However, once I'd built a layout with a backdrop, there was no going back.

STEP 1 Working with styrene

I've used a number of different materials to make backdrops, but I've come to prefer sheet styrene for this task. Styrene is lightweight, and it's easy to

join for smooth-flowing flat or curved surfaces, **2-21**.

While you typically won't find sheet styrene at your local building center, most metropolitan areas have one or more plastics dealers. It is also available online.

While sheet styrene is more expensive than tempered hardboard (I paid $28 per 4 x 8 sheet of .080" white styrene), it has some distinct working advantages. You can roll up a sheet of styrene to fit in almost any automobile. Cutting it is also easy. Just like working with modeling styrene, you simply score and snap the pieces. And if you know the sizes you need when you purchase the material, the dealer will cut them for you at little or no extra cost.

2-21

Gluing styrene strips to the backdrop will reinforce joints.

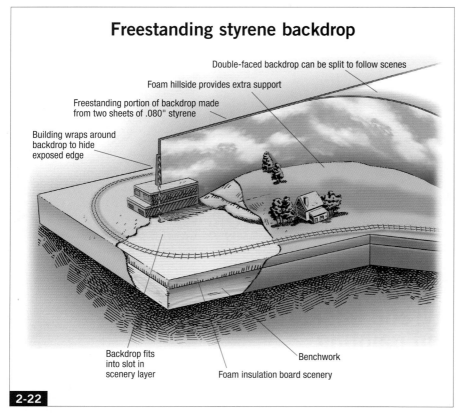

Freestanding styrene backdrop

Double-faced backdrop can be split to follow scenes

Foam hillside provides extra support

Freestanding portion of backdrop made from two sheets of .080" styrene

Building wraps around backdrop to hide exposed edge

Backdrop fits into slot in scenery layer

Benchwork

Foam insulation board scenery

2-22

Illustration by Theo Cobb

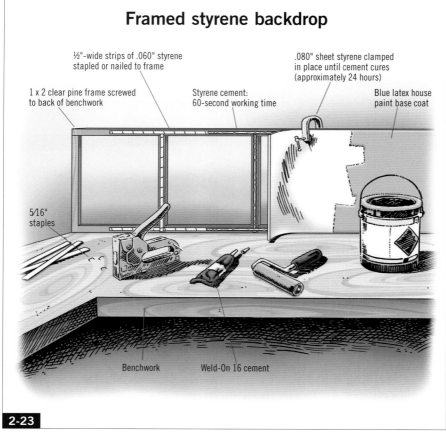

Framed styrene backdrop

½"-wide strips of .060" styrene stapled or nailed to frame

.080" sheet styrene clamped in place until cement cures (approximately 24 hours)

1 x 2 clear pine frame screwed to back of benchwork

Styrene cement: 60-second working time

Blue latex house paint base coat

5⁄16" staples

Benchwork

Weld-On 16 cement

2-23

Illustration by Theo Cobb

Perhaps the best part is that the styrene can be cemented together, just like building a big kit. A 1.5-ounce tube of Weld-On 16 acrylic cement was more than enough to assemble the backdrops for my N scale layout, one-and-a-half 4 x 8 sheets worth.

STEP 2 Using a freestanding styrene backdrop

I used a freestanding styrene backdrop as a view block on one of the peninsulas on my layout, **2-22**. It separates two towns and also hides a staging yard. This backdrop slips into a groove cut into the foam insulation board scenery. Since the backdrop spans two different sections of the layout, I made it removable so the layout would remain portable. Gravity and the foam hold the backdrop in place.

However, .080" styrene, at a height much taller than 16" (the height of this view block), won't stand on its own without leaning. To lend some strength to it, I doubled the thickness of the backdrop by cementing a second sheet along the unsupported side. Where the backdrop curves and intersects other parts of the layout, a single sheet of .080" styrene stands on its own.

To mask the exposed end of the backdrop, I wrapped a building around it.

STEP 3 Making a framed styrene backdrop

Part of my layout runs along the basement wall (painted brick), so building a freestanding backdrop here wasn't practical. Also, I wanted this backdrop to be taller (24"), so I knew I'd need to build a frame for the sheet styrene, **2-23**.

I made the frame from 1 x 2 clear pine. To attach the sheet styrene to the frame without having to fill screw or nail holes in its surface, I first covered the face of the frame with ½"-wide .060" styrene strips, fastening them to the wood using a staple gun and 5⁄16" staples. I then cemented the .080" sheet styrene to the frame with the Weld-On acrylic cement, clamping the styrene in place for 2 hours, until the cement had set.

A word of caution about Weld-On 16 acrylic cement – it sets very quickly when it's exposed to air. You have about 60 seconds to get the parts together! Also, be sure to provide adequate ventilation.

STEP 4 Painting simple clouds

What, you didn't go to art school? Neither did I, and that was perhaps the biggest stumbling block I faced in wanting to add backdrops to my layout. *Model Railroader* has run a number of articles in the past several years that provide great tips, including Mike Danneman's painting story in the October 2004 issue. But if you have a layout where trees, buildings, or hills stand in the foreground in front of the backdrop, you can use this easy method to add blue sky and light clouds without requiring a lot of artistic skill.

Start by painting the backdrop light blue using a latex interior house paint. In choosing a color, the more white it has, the hazier your sky will look. And by adding a bit of gray, you get the look of an overcast day. If you aren't going to move the layout a lot, you don't even need to prime the styrene – the latex paint sticks to it just fine.

Adding clouds is a two-step process. Start by airbrushing the undersides of the clouds Polly Scale L&N Gray, **2-24**. The undersides tend to be shadowed by the rest of the cloud, so they're a bit darker. I add the clouds in two- and three-step layers, making sure to apply them level with the horizon.

Next, airbrush the tops of the clouds using Polly Scale Reefer White, **2-25**. Here you want to build

Power tools

Reciprocating saw and blades

Drill bits

Magnetic screwdriver and bits

Cordless drill and spare battery

Goggles

Though there are many power tools to choose from, you really can build an entire layout with just two – a reciprocating saw and a drill.

Despite the fact that many types of power saws can cut faster, a reciprocating saw (also called a jig saw) offers more versatility as it can make straight, angled, and curved cuts. Thanks to interchangeable blades, the saw can be used to cut wood, plastic, and metal. When selecting a reciprocating saw, look for one with a variable-speed trigger – they are easiest to work with.

The other essential power tool for layout builders is a variable-speed drill. I have a cordless version with a keyless chuck for quickly changing bits. By adding inexpensive driver bits, you can convert a variable-speed drill to a screw gun. I use a magnetic driver bit to hold screws in place on the tip.

When shopping for cordless tools, it's a good idea to pick up a spare rechargeable battery, so the tool is always ready to use. Also, always use proper safety gear, such as eye protection, when working with power tools.

up the clouds in short, level strokes. You want to avoid making a solid white mass. Instead, let some of the blue sky show through, giving your clouds the illusion of fluffiness. Also, be sure to build up all the clouds working from the same end. Nature

works that way, so your backdrop should too.

Don't like some of the results? Brush away the bad clouds with your sky blue paint and start again. Once you've finished, you'll be amazed that adding a cloud-filled sky was this easy. I was!

2-24

After painting the sky blue, airbrush gray lines to form the base for the clouds.

2-25

As you work on the same end, airbrush white in short, level strokes to make the cloud tops.

3-1

CHAPTER THREE

Completing trackwork, wiring, and DCC

At this point in the layout construction process, you're closer to running trains than you might think. Lay a little track, clip the control system to the rails, and you're in business!

Now that you've got the benchwork established and the scenery started, the next step is laying track. To me, tracklaying is one of the most exciting parts of building a model railroad because it doesn't take much track to run your first train, **3-1**. Indeed, hooking up some temporary feeder wires to the rails and running a train over the first few feet of newly laid track is a great idea. Not only does this serve as a test to see if the track is properly installed, it's a motivational boost to keep going – you'll find you want to lay more track as soon as possible, so your trains have someplace to go!

Soon you'll have enough track laid, so you can run more than one train, leading to the next phase – wiring the layout. One of the best developments in the hobby is the growth of DCC. This control system allows for realistic multiple-train operation without extensive electrical work. And DCC offers several options for walkaround train control including easy-to-install wireless radio cabs.

Once the track is in place and wired for operation, you can paint and weather it and add ballast – the first step of adding finished scenery to your layout.

3-2

Laying track for a large yard is easier to do when you solder feeders and preassemble trackwork at your workbench.

PROJECT 1: Laying and wiring track

Trackwork makes or breaks a layout. Good trackwork can actually improve the running characteristics of your locomotives and rolling stock and reward you with years of reliable operation. However, poorly laid track will provide hours of frustration.

With the wealth of high-quality track components available today, laying smooth track isn't difficult. And with the help of a few time-saving techniques, such as soldering feeders and assembling complex trackwork ahead of time at your workbench, even something like a large yard is easy to build, 3-2.

STEP 1 Choosing track and examining wiring methods

For my N scale layout, I chose Peco's line of code 55 track. (Peco makes track for HO and other scales as well.) Rail codes correspond to the rail's height in inches, therefore code 55 rail measures .055" tall.

Peco offers a nice selection of turnouts and specialty pieces such as

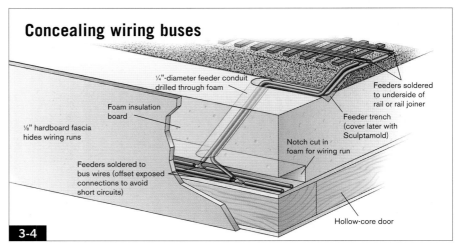

3-3

On Peco turnouts, you can push the factory-installed points, and the spring keeps them in position.

Concealing wiring buses

¼"-diameter feeder conduit drilled through foam

Foam insulation board

⅛" hardboard fascia hides wiring runs

Feeders soldered to bus wires (offset exposed connections to avoid short circuits)

Feeders soldered to underside of rail or rail joiner

Feeder trench (cover later with Sculptamold)

Notch cut in foam for wiring run

Hollow-core door

3-4

Illustration by Jay Smith

27

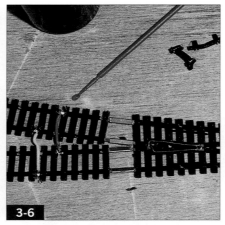

3-5

Soldering feeders to the underside of rail joiners makes them less visible.

3-6

When using live frog turnouts, you need to cut gaps beyond the frog and then add feeders to the inner rails.

3-7

Simple jumper wires can be used in complex track arrangements when using DCC.

Tunnel to wiring run

Wire laid in trench and covered later with Sculptamold

3-8

After the turnout is wired, the wires can be hidden and the turnout cemented to the roadbed.

crossings and turntables. The main reason I chose this track, however, is that Peco turnouts come with a built-in toggle spring for the points. Simply push the points over with your finger, and the spring holds them in position, eliminating the need for manual ground throws or electric switch motors, **3-3**.

I laid the track on top of standard N scale cork roadbed, cemented over the 2" foam subroadbed that was installed in chapter 2. You can use a number of different adhesives to hold the track in place, including carpenter's glue or latex construction adhesives such as Liquid Nails for Projects, but I used ordinary DAP brand latex caulk.

Because I used hollow-core doors for this layout, I devised a slightly unorthodox method to conceal all the wiring. I didn't want any exposed wiring hanging down underneath the door where it could be snagged and damaged. With that in mind, I concealed the wiring buses behind the fascia and inside the scenery, **3-4**.

However, if you're not concerned about snagging wires, you can use more conventional wiring methods: follow all the steps for wiring and laying the track, but run the feeder wires through the door to the underside of the layout. There, you may connect them to the track power bus.

STEP 2 Soldering feeders and jumpers

You can speed up the tracklaying process considerably by preassembling and wiring as much of the trackwork as possible on your workbench. This includes soldering together key track sections, including places where two or more turnouts are in close proximity, and attaching feeder wires.

By soldering feeders to the rails before laying the track, you can attach them to the underside of the rail or rail joiners, **3-5**. This makes the feeders virtually invisible.

I used Peco Electrofrog turnouts on my layout. Unlike insulated frog turnouts where the frog section is electrically dead, an Electrofrog turnout carries current all the way through the frog. This provides smooth locomotive operation through the turnout. Live-frog turnouts require two-rail wiring, which includes cutting gaps in the rails beyond the frog and soldering new feeders to those rails, **3-6**.

If you're using DCC, those extra rail feeders beyond the gaps can be made with simple jumpers, **3-7**. If you're using a DC cab-control system, instead of jumpers, you'll need feeders for each electrically isolated section of rail. For more information about this type of control and two-rail wiring in general, see Andy Sperandeo's book *Easy Model Railroad Wiring*.

Once the turnout is wired, it can be installed on the layout, **3-8**, as described in step 4.

STEP 3 Cutting and filling gaps

When using track components with electrically live frogs, you need to isolate the two rails running away from the frog, opposite the points end. You can do this with plastic rail joiners, but they tend to look unrealistically oversize. Instead, I prefer to cut gaps in the rail at the appropriate points and then fill them with gray ABS plastic.

After laying a turnout and its adjoining track and letting the adhesive caulk dry for 24 hours, use a motor tool with a cutoff disk to cut gaps in the two rails, **3-9**. Be sure to cut these gaps between two ties to keep the rail sections aligned.

Next, place a drop of cyanoacrylate adhesive (CA) into the gaps and then insert .010" strips of gray ABS plastic to fill the spaces, **3-10**. When the CA has dried, use a sharp hobby knife to trim away the excess plastic and file the plug to match the profile of the rail. When you paint this section of track, the plastic is no longer visible.

STEP 4 Working on curves

Flextrack is one of those miracle model railroading products: It's fast and easy to use, and you can curve it to follow just about any right-of-way. Forming smooth joints on continuous curves where one section of flextrack meets the next, however, can be a little tricky unless you know the secret.

To get smooth flextrack joints on curves, start by fitting and cementing the first piece of the curve in place, pinning the track to the roadbed so it

3-9

Use a motor tool with a cutoff disk to cut gaps between the ties to keep rails aligned.

.010" ABS plastic filler

3-10

After the cement dries, trim and file the plastic filler to the rail's shape.

3-11

When cementing flextrack to the roadbed, smooth the adhesive caulk's bead, so it doesn't ooze between the ties.

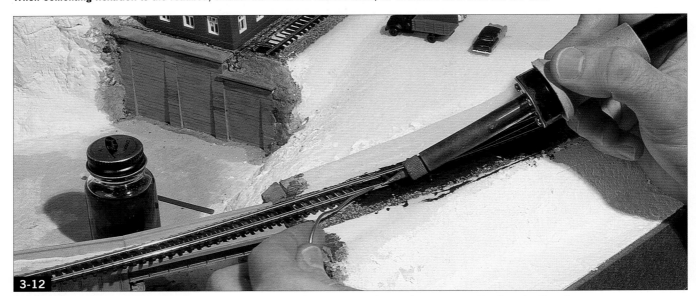

3-12

When adding a second piece of flextrack to form a curve, keep the new section straight as you solder it to the first piece.

3-13

After pressing the flextrack into the adhesive, pin the track to the roadbed to maintain its shape.

can't shift. Next, lay a bead of adhesive caulk for the second piece of the curve, **3-11**. Attach a straight piece of flextrack to the curved section you've already laid and solder the two together, **3-12**.

After letting the solder cool, carefully bend the straight flextrack to follow the curve, pressing it into the adhesive caulk and pinning it in place, **3-13**. Let the adhesive dry overnight. Using this technique, you should be able to lay flextrack on curves, kink free.

By following these steps, you'll be able to lay most any type of trackwork needed to complete your layout.

STEP 5 Adding track bumpers and guardrails

Two additional prototype track details you can add at any time are track bumpers and guardrails.

Track bumpers are a common railroad feature used to keep cars from rolling off the end of the track. A quick look in the Walthers catalog reveals that there are many track bumpers available. I chose metal, Hayes-style bumpers made by Tomar Industries.

These bumpers come soldered to a short section of code 80 track, but that didn't match my existing Peco code 55 rail. For uniform appearance, I removed the bumpers and soldered them to the Peco track, **3-14**.

Because the bumper is solid metal, you'll need to gap one of the rails to prevent a short circuit. I cut the gap and filled it using the same method as described in step 3. Real bumpers are often left unpainted, so I painted mine a nice rust color, **3-15**.

Bridge guardrails are another prototype track feature. I made my guardrails from rail stripped off a piece of Atlas code 55 flextrack (you could also use Micro Engineering code 40 rail).

If you're installing the guardrails after painting and ballasting the track like I did, you'll want to paint them before installation. Cut and bend the rails to fit between your bridge tracks, then spray them a rust color. Cement the guardrails in place with CA, **3-16**. Once the adhesive has set, weather the rail with a wash of thinned black paint to match the rest of your track, **3-17**.

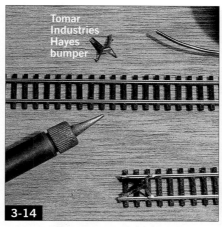

3-14

3-15

A bumper may come installed on a track piece. If it doesn't match your track, remove the bumper and solder it to your rails.

When soldering a bumper to the rails, you must cut a gap in one rail to electrically isolate the bumper.

Guardrail made from Atlas code 55 rail

3-16

Cement guardrails to tie tops with CA, making sure that the ends do not touch to avoid potential short circuits.

3-17

Complete guardrail installation by adding a wash of thinned black paint as weathering.

Digital Command Control (DCC) is an exciting way to realistically run a model railroad.

Tracklaying and wiring tools

Solder

Needlenose pliers

Wire stripper

Soldering iron and station

Rail nipper

Abrasive rail cleaner

NMRA track gauge

Needle files

Jim Forbes

Laying track and wiring a layout requires basic tools, including a needlenose pliers, a wire stripper, and an assortment of small files, as well as some specialized equipment. One special tool is a rail nipper, used to quickly cut rail to size. A rail nipper is designed to cut rail only – using it to cut anything else can damage the cutting surfaces and render the tool useless.

Another specialized tracklaying tool is a track gauge. The one shown is from the National Model Railroad Association (NMRA) and includes features for correctly gauging rails and guard rails and for checking the depth of flangeways for turnout frogs.

Finally, the primary tool for joining wires and attaching them to the rails is a soldering iron. A 25- to 40-watt iron with a pencil tip is sufficient for soldering wires to HO and N scale rail. A soldering station that holds the hot iron and provides a sponge (dampened with water) to clean the tip is also handy to have.

PROJECT 2:
Installing a DCC system

Digital Command Control is a great way to operate a model railroad realistically. When I built the first section of my Naugatuck Valley RR, I wired it for use with an Atlas Commander DCC system. The system was easy to use and offered some room for expansion with walkaround throttles. For a small N scale layout it was ideal.

However, once I'd expanded the layout and started hosting operating sessions, I found I was pushing the limits of what the Atlas system could do. I needed a DCC system that could handle more operators, provide better consisting features (running locomotives in multiple units), and offer easier access to advanced programming options.

After doing some shopping, I chose a Lenz Set 100 as my new DCC system. The choice seemed only natural: the Atlas DCC system uses Lenz's XpressNet protocol, which meant that I could reuse many of my existing Atlas components (the cab bus, plug ports, and all of my Atlas walkaround throttles), **3-18**. If there's a lesson to be learned here, it's this: choose a DCC system that can be upgraded easily.

Even if you don't think you'll ever need a bigger system, it's a good idea to leave yourself that option for the future.

STEP 1 Making basic connections

The Lenz Set 100 includes an LZV100 command/power station and an LH100 master throttle for programming and running trains. The instruction manual provides a list of recommended power supplies. I selected the Digitrax PS515 5A, 15V supply. If you need more power for your layout, you can add Lenz LV102 5A or LV200 10A boosters to your installation – each requires its own power source.

Installing the Lenz Set 100 was pretty much a plug-and-play affair. Lenz components connect to one another by screw terminals, 6-pin RJ-type connectors, or 5-pin DIN connectors. The power supply connects to terminals U and V on the LZV100, **3-19**. The track bus connects to terminals J and K, and the programming track to terminals P and Q. At this point, it's a good idea to test the system. Plug the LH100 into the command station and try running a train.

You can connect the XpressNet cab bus (explained in steps 4-6) to the LZV100 in one of two ways. The first option is to use the 5-pin DIN connector at the back of the LZV100. The Set 100 included a coiled patch cable with a 5-pin DIN connector on one end and an RJ25 connector on the other. To make the link, plug the DIN connector into the command station and the RJ connector into the back of a Lenz LA152 or Atlas 332 XpressNet plug panel on your cab bus, and it's good to go.

The second option is to hard-wire the cable to screw terminals at the back of the LZV100. I chose to do this because I didn't want to try pushing the coiled patch cable through the foam scenery to connect it to the existing cab bus. After stripping the plastic insulation from the 6-wire cable, I stripped the middle four wires, tinned them with solder, and connected them to the LZV100's L, M, A, and B terminals, following the color-code instructions in the Lenz manual. You don't use the outer two wires (white and blue), so I clipped them off.

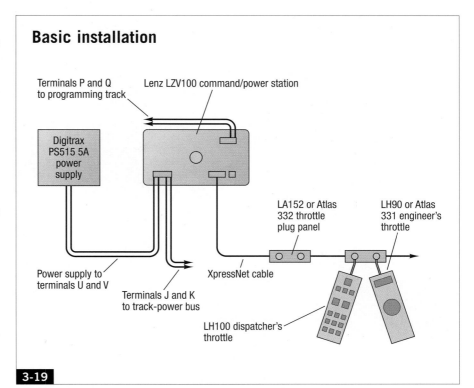

Basic installation

Terminals P and Q to programming track

Lenz LZV100 command/power station

Digitrax PS515 5A power supply

Power supply to terminals U and V

Terminals J and K to track-power bus

LA152 or Atlas 332 throttle plug panel

XpressNet cable

LH90 or Atlas 331 engineer's throttle

LH100 dispatcher's throttle

3-19

Illustration by Theo Cobb

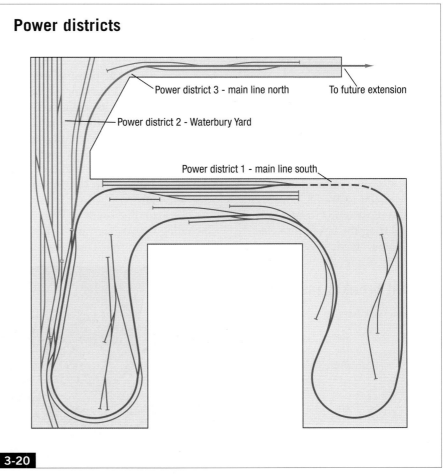

Power districts

Power district 3 - main line north

To future extension

Power district 2 - Waterbury Yard

Power district 1 - main line south

3-20

Illustration by Rick Johnson

PS1 – one circuit breaker

3-21

Circuit breakers can be mounted to the underside of the layout.

STEP 2 Adding power districts

Although DCC allows you to wire a small or midsize model railroad as one big electrical block, that's not a good idea. Any short circuit will trip your DCC system's circuit breaker and shut down power to the entire layout until the short is cleared. While this isn't much of a problem when you're operating the railroad by yourself, if you have additional people running trains (a primary reason to use DCC), a short will cause those trains to stop as well.

By splitting the layout into electrically isolated, circuit-breaker-protected sections called power districts, you can prevent single short circuits from shutting down the entire railroad. Should a short occur in one power district, its breaker trips until the short is cleared, and all other districts remain active.

To add power districts to my layout, I started by identifying traffic patterns. Waterbury Yard has one or more locomotives running in it almost constantly, so I made that its own power district, **3-20**.

The main line south of Waterbury, including the staging yard, typically sees one or two trains operating at a time, so it became the second power district. The main line north from Waterbury forms the third district. Though there isn't much to this part of the layout at the moment, once I complete the next addition, it will be about the same size as the first district.

I used Power Shield circuit breakers from Tony's Train Exchange to protect my three power districts. The breakers are wired between the LZV100 and the track power bus for each district, **3-22**. You can mount the circuit breakers to the underside of the layout, **3-21**.

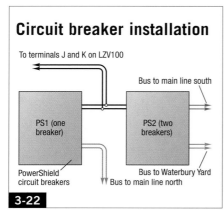

Circuit breaker installation

To terminals J and K on LZV100

Bus to main line south

PS1 (one breaker)

PS2 (two breakers)

PowerShield circuit breakers

Bus to Waterbury Yard

Bus to main line north

3-22

Illustration by Theo Cobb

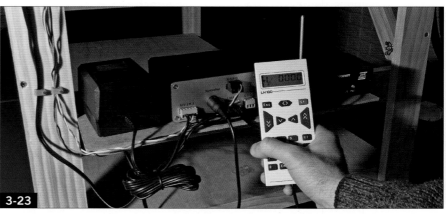

3-23

To program the command station, set the LH100 throttle to locomotive address 0000.

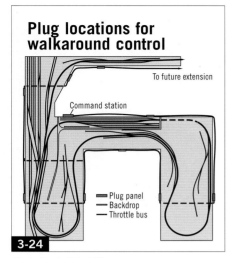

Plug locations for walkaround control

To future extension

Command station

- Plug panel
- Backdrop
- Throttle bus

3-24

Illustration by Robert Wegner

STEP 3 Making adjustments

A great feature of the Lenz LZV100 is that it offers some custom options. My favorite being that you can set the track voltage for the layout. After I'd fired up the Lenz system, I took a reading with a RRamp meter made by DCC Specialties to measure DCC track voltage. The reading was 15.6V. Though this is fine for HO scale trains and decoders, I think it's a bit high when operating N scale locomotives. All decoders give off heat, and inside an N scale locomotive, there's not much room for air movement. With that in mind, I changed the LZV100's output to 13V.

You program the command station by setting the LH100 master throttle to locomotive address 0000, **3-23**. Once you've done that, you need to enter the system's mode for programming-on-the-main (keys F and 7) and change the values for configuration variable (CV) 7.

To get a track output of 13V, I first entered a value of 50 for CV7. I then pushed the Clear button and entered an additional value of 26 for CV7. You must enter the second value within 15 seconds of the first for the change to take effect. Once the new voltage is set, it will remain that way unless you change it or reset the LZV100 to its original configuration.

STEP 4 Installing a cab bus

Although running trains from a fixed location works well on a small layout, on larger model railroads, it's more enjoyable to follow your train, espe-

3-25

Lenz's XpressNet system is compatible with Atlas HandCommand throttles.

cially when performing switching duties. Also, since part of the fun of DCC is being able to easily run more than one train at a time, it only makes sense that you will eventually want more than one throttle, so you can enjoy the layout with friends.

The Lenz system offers the option of adding extra cabs, or throttles. In addition to the LH100 master throttle, Lenz also makes the LH90 operator's throttle, and both work well with the system. However, because I'd originally wired the layout for an Atlas system, I already had several Atlas HandCommand throttles, **3-25**. Since these are made by Lenz and are fully compatible with Lenz's XpressNet system, I decided to use them as my operator throttles.

The HandCommand throttles are strictly operator cabs, having no advance functions or programming capabilities. Though they work great for my application, the Atlas cabs use only 2-digit locomotive addresses and

have access to just five DCC functions. Should you need 4-digit addresses or more functions, you'll want to use the Lenz LH100 or LH90 throttles instead.

Before installing the cab bus and XpressNet plug panels, you should take the time to carefully decide where to put them. Simply placing a panel every six to eight feet around the layout isn't always the best solution, and you may wind up with panels where they aren't needed.

I placed one panel in the middle of each part of my layout that required switching work, **3-24**. With this method, I ended up with a fairly even distribution without buying more panels than were really necessary.

Once you decide where to put your throttle panels, test the location by taping the throttle cord to the fascia. If you can comfortably work at that place on the railroad while still holding the throttle, it's a good location for the panel.

3-26

Lenz and Atlas plug panels connect together with modular 6-wire cables.

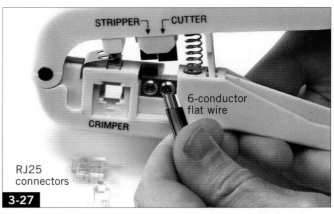

3-27

When stripping data cables, do not remove the insulation from the wires inside the cable.

STEP 5 Making cables

Adding the throttle bus to your layout is as easy as plugging the pieces together. Lenz uses a common 6-wire data cable (included with each Atlas HandCommand and Lenz or Atlas XpressNet panel) to connect the plug panels together, **3-26**.

You can use Lenz cables as is or buy data cables from an electronics supplier, but they'll probably be longer than you need. (Do not use phone cables – they aren't the same.) To shorten the cables, use a data cable crimping tool (available at most hardware stores) and RJ25 6-conductor modular connectors.

To make a cable shorter, first use the cutter on the crimping tool to clip an existing data cable to the correct length. Next, use the tool's built-in stripper to remove the plastic insulation, exposing the six wires, **3-27**. Place an RJ25 connector into the crimping slot and slip the exposed wires into the

back of the connector, making sure the cable is oriented properly. Squeeze the handle to lock the wire permanently into the RJ25 connector, and the cable is ready to use.

When customizing cables, pay special attention to the orientation of the RJ25 connectors – their clips should be on opposite sides of the cable. Flat cable has a seam down one side, making it easy to tell which side you're looking at. If the clip of one RJ25 connector is face up on the seam side, the other connector should have its clip on the smooth side, or the wires will be crossed when you plug it in.

STEP 6 Installing panels

Once you have the cables ready, all that remains is to cut the panel holes in the fascia, connect the throttle bus together, and fasten the panels in place.

The XpressNet panels include a template for cutting the fascia, **3-28**. (On my layout, the fascia is ⅛" hard-

board.) After marking the locations, cut the holes using a reciprocating saw, and vacuum the sawdust when finished. Test-fit the panel to make sure it fits properly, then mark and drill the mounting holes.

Before attaching the panels to the fascia, test them. Clip the throttle bus cables into the back of all the panels and connect the XpressNet bus on the LZV100 command station (see step 1). Turn on the DCC system to make sure the panels work properly, **3-29**. Each panel has a green pilot light, and if data is being transmitted and received properly, it will be lit. If all lights are green, screw the panels in place, and you're ready to run your railroad with DCC walkaround control.

STEP 7 Going wireless

Though my collection of tethered Atlas and Lenz throttles works just fine, certain jobs that have to travel the layout's entire main line, such as the

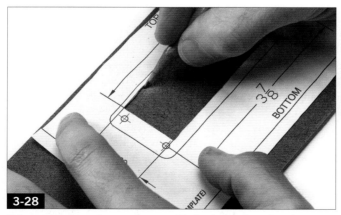

3-28

Using a template when cutting panel holes in fascia makes for an accurate fit.

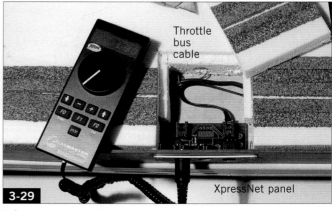

3-29

This layout cutaway shows proper panel installation.

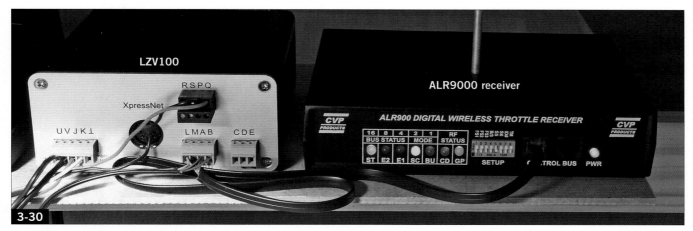

3-30

The ALR9000 receiver plugs into the XpressNet bus and needs no external power supply.

commuter trains, could really benefit from having wireless cabs to keep the crews from getting tangled up with each other. With that in mind, I added a CVP Products ALR900 receiver module and an RF1300 throttle to the Lenz system.

The ALR900 simply plugs into the XpressNet bus. I chose to wire it into the L, M, A, B terminals on the LZV100, **3-30**. The ALR900 needs no external power supply, as it's powered via the XpressNet connection. The RF1300 throttle uses four AAA batteries. To work with the Lenz LZV100 command station, the ALR900 must have its operating switch no. 5 set to On. All others should be in the Off position.

Lenz's XpressNet can handle 31 input devices, the most common being cabs. Each device needs to have its own ID number to work properly, including the Atlas and Lenz cabs and the CVP RF1300 throttles. You can find the procedure for setting the ID number (1 through 31) for each input item in its respective instruction manual.

After setting the ID for a cab, I write its number on the top of the case with a white paint pen, so I know which numbers I've used.

STEP 8 Hanging throttles (optional)

Adding some way to hang your throttles on your layout is a good idea. When I first installed my DCC system, I used self-adhesive strips of hook-and-loop fasteners to hang up the cabs. I placed hook strips (the soft material) on the back of the throttle and the loop strips on the layout's fascia near the plug ports. While this worked for a while, the adhesive let go after prolonged use.

As a more reliable solution, I added a simple screw eye to each cab, mounting the eye to the top of the plastic case. The screw eye then slips over a smooth-plastic, light-duty hook, **3-31**. I attached the hooks to the layout with round-head wood screws. Hooks that have rounded edges are less likely to catch on clothing as operators and visitors walk by.

3-31

Hanging throttles on a layout prevents cords from tangling and keeps throttles in easy reach for operators.

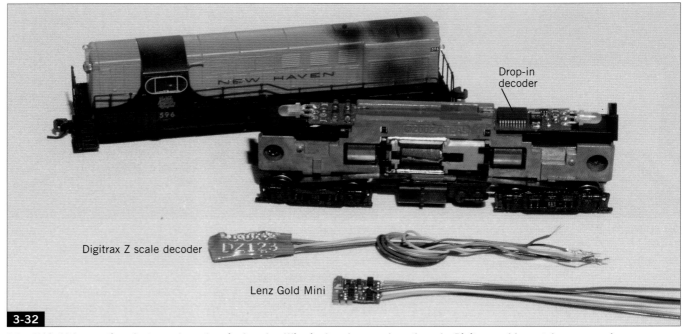

Drop-in decoder

Digitrax Z scale decoder

Lenz Gold Mini

3-32

Atlas H16-44 locomotives feature a Lenz drop-in decoder. Wire-in decoders, such as those by Digitrax and Lenz, take more work.

PROJECT 3: Installing decoders in N scale locomotives

A key component to Digital Command Control is the mobile decoder, the means by which the DCC system communicates with each engine on your layout. Every locomotive used on a DCC layout will need a decoder.

If you're modeling in HO scale, most manufacturers either include factory-installed DCC decoders in their locomotives, or they offer an easy way to install one by using plugs. N scale

modelers, however, are not quite as lucky. Though more manufacturers now offer N scale locomotives factory-equipped with decoders, the majority of the models on the market require some modification to isolate the motor and include space for a decoder.

There are two options for do-it-yourself decoder installation in N scale models – drop-in and wired-in. Drop-in decoders are just as the name implies. After removing the shell from the model, you remove the engine's circuit board (wedged between the two halves of the frame) and replace it with a DCC decoder designed to fit in that location. Most drop-in installations can be completed in a few minutes, and both Lenz and Digitrax

make these decoders for N scale models, **3-32**.

Unfortunately, not every N scale locomotive is designed to accommodate drop-in decoders. Many N scale engines, particularly older models, need to have the frame modified to electrically isolate the motor. The decoder is then wired in place using soldered connections. Thanks to Aztec Manufacturing, this isn't as difficult as it may sound.

For a small fee, Aztec will mill a space for a decoder in your locomotive frame and isolate the motor. Simply follow the instructions on the company's Web site, www.aztectrains.com, and drop your locomotive frame in the mail. Aztec's service is fast (about 10 days), and unlike using replacement frames, once the milling is finished, you're still using the locomotive's original frame. **3-33**. This means that the motor and gears will fit properly.

Aztec also includes decoder installation instructions with each milled frame, including information on cutting the decoder's wires to the correct length. Digitrax, Lenz, and NCE Corporation all make decoders that work well in this type of application. For more detailed information about installing and programming DCC decoders, see Mike Polsgrove's book *DCC Projects and Applications*.

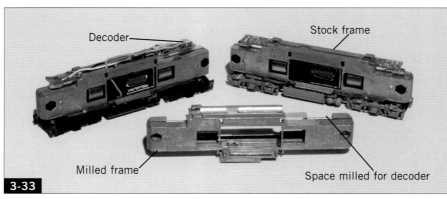

Decoder

Stock frame

Milled frame

Space milled for decoder

3-33

An Atlas GP9 frame (right) is milled by Aztec (center) and then reassembled with a decoder installed (left).

3-34

Painting your track hides its metallic and plastic shine and, together with ballasting, adds realism to your trackwork.

3-35

A typical stretch of railroad track shows various colors and weathering.

PROJECT 4:
Making your track realistic

Your track is every bit as much a model as the trains that run on it are. Often, however, painting, ballasting, and weathering trackwork is overlooked by modelers. I've seen a number of layouts that feature beautifully detailed trains running on track that looks like it just came from the hobby shop, spoiling the sense of realism.

The truth is that railroads are big, dirty industries. A careful look at even

the best-maintained right-of-way will clearly reveal rusty rails, grimy ties, and oily deposits along the ballast – details that can easily be added to most flextrack and ready-made turnouts using acrylic modeling paints and an airbrush.

Though detailing your track may seem like a fair amount of work, a little goes a long way, and you can greatly improve your track's overall appearance by painting and ballasting it, 3-34.

STEP 1 Painting ties and rails

Painting your track to hide its metallic and plastic shine is a simple step, and it makes your right-of-way look

a lot more like the real thing. The best research is done by looking at the prototype. Railroad tracks are a combination of various shades of brown, black, and gray, depending on region of the country and financial state of the railroad. Typically, older lines that need some maintenance have bright orange, rusty rail and faded gray ties, 3-35. Well-manicured main lines have newer, dark brown or sometimes bluish-black ties and rich brown rail.

For the Naugatuck Valley, I chose to airbrush the track and rail a unifying base-coat mixture of three parts Polly Scale Roof Brown plus one part Engine Black. Before you begin air-

3-36

Be sure to airbrush both sides of the rails and protect switch points and hinges.

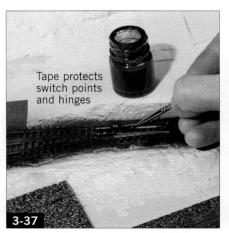

3-37

Carefully brush paint where the rails were taped and avoid painting where the point and stock rail meet.

3-38

Use an abrasive block to clean paint off the rail tops before it cures.

3-39

I painted the edges of the right-of-way with a flat black latex house paint before ballasting the track.

3-40

With a teaspoon, sift the ballast gently into the glue mixture, which is nine parts white glue thinned with one part water.

Ballast soaked with rubbing alcohol

3-41

In the final ballasting step, apply rubbing alcohol to the ballast with a pipette and then add scenery cement, so the cement shows between the stones.

brushing, however, take a few moments to mask off your switch points and hinges and any important landscape features, such as roads. Switch points and hinges, in particular, need special care and attention, so they still conduct electricity once you've finished painting.

After applying the base coat of paint, I sprayed a weathering coat of Polly Scale L&N Gray, thinned 50 percent, over small groups of ties along the track to give the impression that some ties are older than others, 3-36.

STEP 2 Cleaning up, round I

Once you've airbrushed a section of trackwork, you can pull the tape off the switch points and hinges and carefully brush-paint the rails and ties, 3-37. I keep a small bottle of custom-mixed rail paint for this purpose, so it matches the airbrushed coat. Avoid flowing paint between the point and stock rails or into the hinge. If you get any paint in these areas, clean it out immediately. Paint allowed to dry in these areas will cause electrical contact problems.

Once you've finished the touch-up painting, use an abrasive block, such as Bright Boy, to clean the paint off the rail tops, 3-38. If you allow paint on the rails to dry completely, it will be very difficult to clean off later.

After scrubbing, I vacuum the track to remove any abrasive residue and dried paint crumbs.

STEP 3 Painting the scenery base

Before you can start ballasting, you need to give the scenery surrounding the track a base coat of paint. I modeled the Naugatuck Valley RR after the New Haven in the 1950s, when it was common practice to cover the ground surrounding the track with cinders and gravel to promote drainage and prevent vegetation from growing along the tracks. To simulate this, I use dark gray cinder ballast (shown in step 4). Painting the scenery underneath the cinder areas a dark color helps the material look better.

I used flat black latex house paint, brushing it along both sides of the tracks and in any area that would be covered with cinders, such as part of the depot parking lot, **3-39**. If you have some of the surrounding scenery ready, you may want to paint it a tan base color at this time (see chapter 4). Once the paint dries, you're ready to begin ballasting.

STEP 4 Bringing on the ballast

My dressing ballast (top layer) for the main line is Woodland Scenics Light Gray Fine Ballast. For the fill along the main line and all the ballast on spurs, I use Highball Products N scale cinders. Ballasting can be tricky business because the little stones like to go just about everywhere except where you want them. You can simplify these ballast-control issues by dividing the work into three basic steps.

Start by brushing a small amount of white glue, diluted 10 percent with water, along the sloped sides of the roadbed. Then, using a teaspoon, gently sift the ballast into the wet glue, **3-40**. The thicker glue mixture helps the ballast stay in place along the slope when it is soaked with scenery cement in the final step.

Using the teaspoon again, now sift ballast between the rails. A little goes a long way here, so don't use too much. Gently clean the ballast off the tops of the ties and out of the rail's web with a small paintbrush.

Finally, add cinders along the outer edge of the dressed ballast. Brush a new path of diluted white glue along the outer edges of the roadbed slope and sift the cinder material into the glue.

As a final step, soak the ballast with rubbing alcohol, applied with a pipette. While the ballast is still wet, slowly dribble on Woodland Scenics scenery cement, **3-41**. The alcohol allows the scenery cement to wick its way between the ballast stones without disturbing them, but then it evaporates quickly, leaving the cement to hold everything together. How much cement do you need? You don't want too much to wash the ballast off the right-of-way, but you should be able to see it oozing between the stones.

STEP 5 Cleaning up, round II

When the ballast has had a day to dry, it's time to clean the track. Try as

3-42

Make sure that the points and hinges are clean and that the flangeways and frog are clear of ballast. Rolling a test car through those areas makes finding stray ballast easy.

3-43

After spraying a weathering coat down the center of the track between the rails, clean the rail tops before the paint dries.

you may to keep the ballast out of places like switch points and flangeways, it seems to always find them. I use an assortment of small tools for this cleaning project, including a track-cleaning block, a hobby knife, an old toothbrush, and a test car, **3-42**.

The easiest way to find sections of track that need to be cleared of ballast is to roll a freight car along the track with your finger. Every place that the car bumps along the rails should be checked and cleared of ballast. Once you've cleaned a section of track, vacuum up any loose material, so it can't wedge itself into another problem spot later.

STEP 6 Weathering track

When the ballasted track is operating trouble-free, I use my airbrush to spray the center line of the track with a weathering streak, **3-43**. This represents the oil and grime that collects on the track and ballast from passing trains. My weathering coat is a very thin mixture of Polly Scale Grimy Black diluted with rubbing alcohol.

After that, I clean the rail tops one last time and then run a train over the new section of freshly modeled trackwork. Now that the trackwork is finished, it's time to think about adding the rest of the scenery as well as the towns and industries that your railroad serves.

4-1

CHAPTER FOUR

Constructing scenery

Without trees, grass, and hills, a model railroad would simply be track tacked to bare plywood. Detailed scenery brings a model world to life.

Scenery is what makes a model railroad believable. Rocks, hills, trees, and rivers are the elements that take a layout beyond being a nice collection of scale model trains, **4-1**. Common features like pine trees or prairie grasses that merely subsist in the background of everyday life are, incredibly, the catalyst for transforming a model railroad into a miniature world.

As with any part of the hobby, you can't build picture-perfect scenery without some practice and patience. I've had my share of "do-overs," and I've known several modelers who have gone back and torn out the first sections of scenery they'd built because they'd learned so much more by the time they got to the other end of the railroad. That's actually a pretty common occurrence, and it's the great part of doing scenery work. Like what you did? Keep doing it. Don't like it? Rip it out and try again.

The best part of making scenery is that there are examples of it all around you. Emulate what nature does, and you are on your way to building a great looking layout.

4-2

Rubber rock molds from manufacturers such as Woodland Scenics are formed from real rocks to help reproduce sharp details, such as the eroded faces on these outcroppings.

PROJECT 1:
Casting rocks

Nothing says "impressive" quite like a rugged mountain range full of jagged rock faces. Though mountains appear solid to us, many are just individual layers of rocks, stacked one on top of another. If you keep this idea in mind, then adding impressive rock features to your layout is not a difficult task, **4-2**. Whether you need a whole mountainside or just one or two outcroppings along a cut or low hill, making rock features is actually quite easy. Thanks to readily available materials such as Hydrocal plaster and rubber rock molds, you can cast your own highly detailed rocks and add a little mountain majesty to your layout.

STEP 1 Using rock molds

One of the easiest ways to create realistic rocks for your layout is to cast your own formations out of Hydrocal. This is a fine type of plaster that's easy to use, becomes lightweight when dry, and

reproduces sharp details well. These properties, along with the fact that it's easy to color, make Hydrocal an ideal choice for molding projects.

To form the rocks themselves, you can use rubber molds. A number of manufacturers offer molds in a variety of sizes and shapes. These molds produce realistic results because they are usually formed from actual rocks. They are also inexpensive and can be used repeatedly with proper care – some of my molds are more than 15 years old and still going strong.

You can also make your own molds from latex rubber or other materials. One easy alternative molding method is described on page 45.

Casting rocks is a relatively fast project and a lot of fun. There are two common methods – straight casting and casting in place – and each has its own advantages. Straight casting is a little easier than casting in place. It simply means that you cast the rock, let the plaster harden, and remove it from the mold to use later, **4-3**.

Casting in place requires a little

4-3

When casting rocks, mixing tools, Hydrocal plaster, and molds produce good results.
Bill Zuback

more finesse. In this method, as the plaster starts to set, you press the mold onto the layout while the rock casting is still soft. This allows you to wrap the rock around unusual shapes. Once the plaster sets (about 30 minutes), you can remove the mold.

4-4

When straight casting, first wet the mold with water to help the soupy plaster mix fill in the fine details of the mold. *Bill Zuback*

4-5

Peel away the mold when the casting is firm and cool to the touch. *Bill Zuback*

STEP 2 Casting rocks

In this step, I'll explain the straight casting method. First, mix a small amount of Hydrocal with water in a container until the plaster has a soupy (not runny) consistency. Be careful that you don't add too much water, or the plaster won't set properly.

Next, wet the rubber mold with water to help the plaster work its way into the mold's details, **4-4**. You can use a misting bottle or simply run the mold briefly under the tap and shake off the excess liquid. The mold should be damp but not so wet that water pools in the bottom. Set the wet rubber mold on a level surface and fill it with Hydrocal.

You don't get a lot of working time with casting plaster. I used Woodland

Scenics Lightweight Hydrocal (no. C1201), which has a working time of about five minutes. The material sets up in 30 to 40 minutes. As the Hydrocal sets, it produces heat. Once the Hydrocal is cool to the touch, remove it by peeling the mold away from the plaster, **4-5**. Leave the casting to cure overnight.

Throw any excess plaster in the trash (don't dump it down the sink) and wash off your tools. You can clean excess plaster from the rubber mold by flexing it.

STEP 3 Installing castings

Installing the castings on the layout is simply a matter of gluing them to the scenery with a construction adhesive or latex caulk, **4-6**. For making larger rock formations, cut and piece together two

or more castings. Hydrocal is easy to cut with a razor saw or utility knife, **4-7**, and you can score and snap the pieces apart if you're making straight cuts. I made the rock outcropping shown in photo **4-2** by cutting one casting in half.

If you don't have a lot of rock molds and need to make a bigger outcropping, you can use the same castings over and over. To make them look different, turn one or two castings upside down or stagger their positions on the hillside. Because many geological features have repeating patterns, this simple trick gives your rock formation a connected appearance without looking out of place.

Once you've glued the castings to the layout, fill in any gaps with Sculptamold or more Hydrocal, **4-8**.

4-6

Use construction adhesive or latex caulk to glue castings to scenery.

4-7

When making larger rock formations, castings can be easily cut using a razor saw.

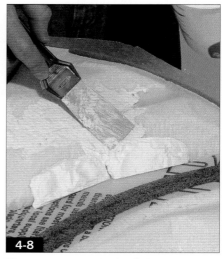

4-8

Wax paper protects the fascia from excess Sculptamold or Hydrocal when filling in gaps.

STEP 4 Coloring rocks

There are many different ways to paint rocks, and working from photos of real rocks is a great help when choosing colors. I prefer staining Hydrocal castings with thinned washes of acrylic paint. To stain the rocks, start with lighter colors and add darker colors as each layer dries. For this project, I used Polly Scale Mud as a base coat, but you may want to pick colors that match those from the region you're modeling.

Using an artist's paintbrush, daub some base-coat paint onto a mixing palette, such as the lid to a cottage-cheese container, **4-9**. Next, add water to the paint until you've thinned the color substantially, making a runny stain. Liberally apply the stain to the rocks and let it dry. If the color is too dark and you want to lighten it, dab the surface with a paper towel while the stain is still wet. This will pull some of the pigment off the casting.

To add shadows that accent the cracks and crevices, apply a separate wash of darker stain. In this case, I used Roof Brown. Mix a stain from the acrylic paint as you did the lighter base coat and then apply it to the rock surface. Instead of using a lot of stain, however, this time you just want to dribble a little in the recesses of the rock or apply a light wash over larger surfaces. Again, if you think the color is too dark, dab the area with a paper towel to draw off the pigment.

4-9

Mix paint on a plastic container lid when matching the color of the real rocks you are modeling.

STEP 5 Making easy, do-it-yourself rock molds (optional)

Want to make unique rock castings? Here's an interesting method discovered by MR's editor Terry Thompson. Play-Doh modeling compound is a great one-time mold-making material. It's water-soluble, easy to work with, and reproduces crisp details when used with Hydrocal.

After choosing a rock to copy, knead a ball of Play-Doh until the material is soft and pliable. Press the dough onto a flat surface, making a disk about ¾" thick. Next, press the rock you wish to copy into the surface of the dough and carefully remove it, **4-10**. Play-Doh likes to stick to porous materials, so you may need to peel

the mold off the rock. If this happens, carefully flatten the dough back onto the work surface.

Next, use some additional Play-Doh to form edges around the mold. Mix the Hydrocal as before and pour it into the mold. After an hour, gently peel as much of the Play-Doh away from the casting as you can and then let the Hydrocal cure for 48 hours.

Clean the casting by moving it under running water and scrubbing it gently with a toothbrush, **4-11**. Play-Doh hardens after being out of the can for a day or more, so it crumbles and can be brushed off the casting fairly easily. Once the Hydrocal casting is dry, you can glue it to the layout and paint it like any other rock casting.

4-10

Press a real rock into Play-Doh to form a mold and then pour Hydrocal into the mold to create a detailed casting. *Bill Zuback*

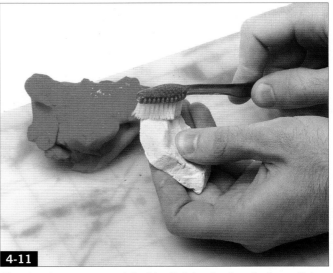

4-11

After the plaster cures and the Play-Doh has hardened, clean off the Play-Doh bits with a toothbrush. *Bill Zuback*

Sheet styrene provides a smooth surface, so it can be used to model roads, driveways, and sidewalks.

PROJECT 2:
Paving Easy Street with styrene

Just as your trains need tracks, your vehicles need roads. After all, building a model railroad layout is all about modeling transportation systems. To that end, our model streets and sidewalks should be given a degree of care similar to what we give our railroad right-of-way.

There are many different types of roads, and depending upon the era you model, their size and construction will vary. One of my favorite road-building materials is ordinary sheet styrene. You can use sheet styrene to simulate both asphalt and concrete surfaces, as well as sidewalks, **4-12**.

Styrene is ideal for streets because it provides a smooth surface, is flexible enough to follow scenic contours, and can be finished in a number of different ways. I use .040" styrene for streets in both HO and N scale. This thickness cuts easily with a hobby knife or scissors but is stiff enough to make smooth transitions over small bumps in the scenery without needing much leveling.

STEP 1 Cutting and scoring

Most of the roads on my N scale 1950s New England-themed layout are concrete, but the method described here works for asphalt roads as well. Simply skip the scribing step and paint the road a shade of gray (not black). I made my rural roads 1¾" wide and my city streets 2¼" wide to allow for curb-side parking.

To make sections of straight road, cut .040" styrene into uniform strips using the score-and-snap technique. With a straightedge as a guide, score the styrene by making several passes with the back of a sharp hobby knife. Next, bend the sheet along your score line – the road piece will snap off with a clean edge.

For curved sections, make a paper pattern of the road first, then trace it onto the styrene with a sharp pencil. Cut the curve from the sheet with a pair of heavy-duty scissors.

If you're making a concrete road, you'll need to add expansion joints, **4-13**. For a guide, I used a section of road that came with a Rix Products N scale concrete highway overpass kit. The Rix road has one expansion joint that runs down the middle, dividing it into two equal-sized lanes, and then is split into even ¹⁵⁄₁₆" sections. To make measuring and scoring these joints easier, I made my sections 1" long.

.040" styrene sheet

Rix street section

Cutting mat with 1" grid

For making expansion joints on N scale concrete roads, I made 1" sections for simpler measuring and scoring.

4-14

You can cement the styrene to the layout with construction adhesive or latex caulk.

4-15

Keep shoulders below the road surface. The grade crossings are from a Blair Line kit.

Again using a straightedge, scribe the center joint first, making a single pass with a hobby knife. Next, scribe the cross joints. I used the 1" grid on my cutting mat as a guide to speed up the process.

STEP 2 Installing streets and shoulders

After you've cut and scored your road sections, test-fit them on the layout. Now is the time to make sure you don't need any extra filing to get a good fit. Gaps between road sections may not be that noticeable in larger scales, but they stand out in N scale.

Attach the road sections to the layout with a construction adhesive or latex caulk. Lay several beads of adhesive along the road's path, then smooth the glue with a putty knife. Starting at one end (usually the last section laid), place a road section on the layout and press

it into the adhesive, **4-14**. Immediately clean up any adhesive that oozes out the sides, so it won't interfere with later scenery work or get on the road surface.

If you're laying the road over a contoured surface, you'll need to pin it in place overnight. I use Woodland Scenics T pins.

After the adhesive has dried for 24 hours, remove the pins and add the shoulders. I use Sculptamold for shoulders, applying it with a putty knife just below the road surface, **4-15**. If you pile up the shoulders too high, you'll run into trouble later when you apply gravel or other scenery materials – the shoulders will sit higher than the road and look out of place.

I added sidewalks in some places, using Evergreen no. 14516 sidewalk sheets, **4-12**. The .040"-thick styrene sheet comes scribed with ¼" squares, saving a lot of work. Simply cut the

sidewalk to size and cement it on top of the road with plastic cement. Be sure to add extra width to your road sections in the places where you'll be installing sidewalks.

STEP 3 Painting

Before painting the road, lightly sand it with fine-grit sandpaper. This will help smooth out any irregularities where sections join and remove ridges at the expansion lines caused by the hobby knife blade.

Painting the streets is a three-step process: airbrushing the base color, applying a wash of black acrylic paint to bring out the expansion lines, and airbrushing several weathering coats of paint to simulate tire paths. You can complete all the painting steps in one evening if you use acrylic paints.

First, airbrush Polly Scale Concrete on the roads as a base coat. The initial

4-16

Lightly sand the road surface with fine sandpaper before airbrushing with Polly Scale Concrete base coat.

4-17

Expansion joints will stand out if washed with black acrylic paint diluted with rubbing alcohol.

4-18

Use an airbrush to make the dark streaks typical of tire paths.

4-19

Striping curved center lines by using a French curve and an extra-fine-point paint pen adds a finishing touch to roads.

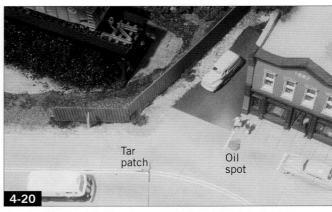

4-20

Tar patch

Oil spot

For final details, you can add tar patches with a Sharpie marker and oil spots with thinned paint.

coat of paint should be even but not so heavy that it fills the scored expansion lines, **4-16**. Two coats applied with an airbrush should work fine.

Next, apply a wash of black acrylic paint, thinned about 95 percent with rubbing alcohol, to make the expansion joints stand out. Brush the wash over the road liberally and then blot off the excess with a paper towel, **4-17**.

For the final step, use a fine setting on your airbrush and slowly build up the tire tracks with a black acrylic paint thinned 50 percent. To lighten the overall appearance of the road, I airbrushed it with a dusting of Polly Scale L&N Gray thinned 50 percent, **4-18**. Let the paint dry overnight before proceeding.

STEP 4 Finishing the scene

You can add street markings (stripes) and simulated tar patches by drawing them on the road surface with markers or paint pens.

To mark the white center lines (later eras would use yellow), I used an extra-fine, opaque white paint pen (available at most office supply stores).

To make straight lines, use a 12" or longer strip of .080" x ½" styrene as a guide. When working with a paint pen, rest the metal part of the pen tip against the straightedge at a slight angle, keeping the painting tip away from where the guide meets the road.

Be careful not to touch the tip to the edge of the styrene guide strip where it meets the pavement. Capillary action will cause the paint to seep under the edge and make a mess. Fortunately, the paint doesn't dry immediately, so have a paper towel and rubbing alcohol handy to wipe away mistakes.

For tight curves, use an artist's French curve tool, **4-19**. When making broader curves, have an assistant bend a strip of styrene along the line's path while you mark it with the paint pen.

To add a little more detail, I used a black, fine-point Sharpie marker to add a few tar patches, **4-20**.

Now you're ready to fill in the scenery around your road, add some signs, and let those vehicles roam the layout uninhibited!

Scenery tools

Caulk gun
Toothbrush
Putty knife
Spray bottle
Razor saw
Pipette
Paint brushes
Sanding blocks
Glass measuring cup

Scenery-construction tools vary based on the method used by the modeler. Since I work primarily with foam insulation board (chapter 2), my scenery tools include a caulk gun for applying construction adhesive and a razor saw and sanding blocks for carving and shaping the foam.

For working with plaster, Sculptamold, and similar products, I use a small putty knife and a one-quart measuring cup as a mixing container. The glass measuring cup makes cleanup easier as plaster doesn't readily adhere to the glass unless it's left to harden overnight.

To paint the scenery layer and apply water-soluble adhesives, I keep an assortment of paintbrushes handy. For applying liquids such as rubbing alcohol or thinned white glue, I use a spray bottle and a plastic eyedropper or pipette. A toothbrush cleans ballast off rails and out of turnout frogs.

I've used my tools to build at least three model railroads. With proper care and cleaning after each use, even scenery construction tools should last a long time.

When completed in layers, building scenery is a manageable process.

PROJECT 3: Providing easy ground cover

Building good-looking scenery can be as easy as any other model railroading project if you simply work in small, manageable steps. My favorite approach to scenery construction is building in layers to form a finished landscape. Some of the most visible layers like grass, shrubs, and trees are actually final steps of scenery work, **4-21**. They aren't added until other layers such as rocks, roads, and basic ground cover are in place.

STEP 1 Applying a base coat

Before breaking out the scenery materials, you need to give the terrain a base coat of paint. Along with sealing the foam, plaster, and Sculptamold used to form the landscape, the paint also provides an even-colored base for applying ground cover. For base coating, I use inexpensive flat interior latex house paint, **4-22**. A medium-tan color works well for general scenery work, though for areas that represent plowed fields or are covered with cinders, I use dark gray or black. Light tan is good for dry riverbeds or gravel roads.

I paint with good-quality synthetic brushes. You shouldn't paint over plaster-cast rocks or bridge abutments as you

won't be able to color them with water-base stains later. I usually color plaster land features first, before completing the surrounding scenery, to avoid staining the completed ground cover.

Though some modelers add a scenery layer to the wet paint, I prefer an approach that allows more control. I let the paint dry thoroughly (overnight) to avoid having the base color bleed into completed scenery features such as roads, plaster rocks, or track ballast.

STEP 2 Applying thick glue

The key to low-mess scenery work is in the adhesives you use. For years, I worked only with diluted white glue and spent a lot of time cleaning up puddles

4-22

As a base coat, a medium-tan, flat interior latex house paint works well for general scenery areas.

(labels in image: Track ballasted ahead of time; Gaps filled with Sculptamold; Fascia removed before working with scenery materials)

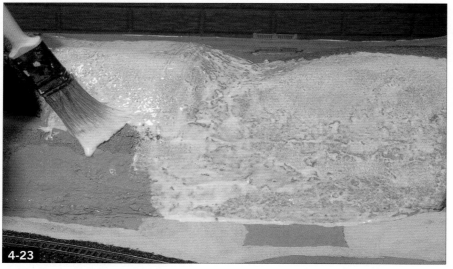

4-23

Thick glue, nine parts glue thinned with one part water, should brush on smoothly yet stay in place with minimal running and pooling.

4-24

Brush glue only where the road will be and use a plastic spoon to apply the gravel.

(labels in image: Silica sand used for road gravel; Ballast container)

from the floor and reworking ground cover that had floated away. Recently, I switched to a method that uses both a thick glue and a thinned glue. This combination of adhesives keeps scenery materials in place while wet and reduces the potential for messy drips.

Before applying scenery materials, such as ground foam or gravel, I brush a coat of thick glue (white glue thinned slightly with water) onto the scenery surface. To make the thick glue, mix approximately nine parts white glue with one part water. Add only enough water to give the glue a latex-paint consistency. When brushed on the surface, the thick glue should cover smoothly without running, 4-23.

After I apply the ground cover materials (see steps 3 and 5) to the thick glue, I soak the area with thinned glue, as explained in step 4.

STEP 3 Making gravel roads and paths

Fine materials such as dirt, ballast, and silica sand look best when applied over smooth surfaces. As a result, I recommend that you start working in places where you'll be using these materials, including gravel roads, parking lots, trails, and industrial yards.

To make a gravel road, begin by lightly marking the road location on the layout with a pencil. Next, using a small art brush, paint the path with the thick glue mixture from step 2. Because the glue dries fairly quickly, don't try to do too much at once. After you've coated a small area with glue, sift the gravel material onto the surface with a spoon. Repeat the process until the road is completely covered, 4-24. Vacuum up any excess gravel from the surface of the road and the surrounding area and apply the thinned glue as explained in step 4. Let the finished road dry overnight before adding any surrounding scenery.

If you wish to give your gravel road an overgrown look, sprinkle a small amount of ground foam down the middle of the wet road.

STEP 4 Soaking with thin glue

The second part of the gluing process is what I call the soaking phase. To stay put on the layout, ground cover materials need to be permeated with adhesive, and that's where the soaking comes in. The soaking step can be completed at any time, but it works best if the thick glue from the previous step is still tacky.

I begin by lightly misting the ground cover with a 50/50 mixture of rubbing alcohol and water from a spray bottle. Unlike pure water, the alcohol and water mix penetrates ballast, dirt, and ground foam well and doesn't bead up on the surface. Be careful not to use too much of the diluted alcohol. You want the scenic material to be damp, not sopping wet, so it will stay in place and the glue distributes evenly.

Next, I apply a small amount of Woodland Scenics premixed Scenic Cement to the damp area using an eyedropper (Testor's pipettes work great), 4-25. As it goes on, Scenic Cement is a milky-white color, making it easy to see where you've applied it, but then dries clear like white glue. However, avoid letting the cement dry on any open surfaces such as rocks, concrete roads, and retaining walls – it can leave an unwanted glossy shine on objects with a flat finish.

4-25

Carefully apply the scenery cement to rock debris to avoid damaging the rock castings.

If you wind up with puddles from too much cement or diluted alcohol, dip the edge of a paper towel into the pooled material to wick away the excess liquid, leaving the scenery materials undisturbed.

Because you're dealing with thinned liquids, it's a good idea to take some extra precautions in this step. I remove the fascia, place a plastic drop cloth under the layout, and pin a strip of folded paper towels along the edge to catch any drips, 4-26.

You can use this two-part gluing process with all other materials, including ballast, ground foam, and even dirt.

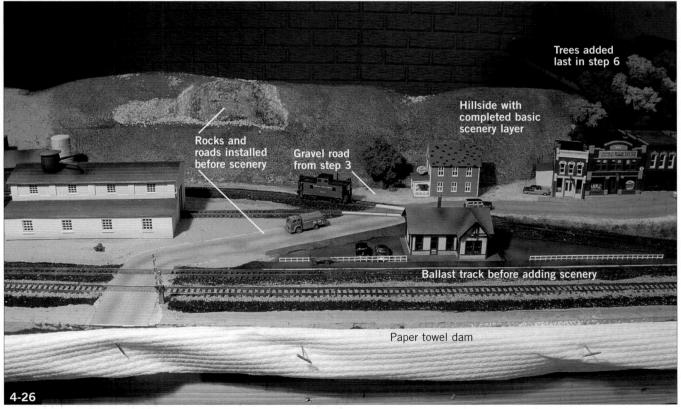

Trees added last in step 6

Hillside with completed basic scenery layer

Rocks and roads installed before scenery

Gravel road from step 3

Ballast track before adding scenery

Paper towel dam

4-26

Building model railroad scenery is completed in a number of stages.

4-27

After applying thick glue, sprinkle on ground foam and vacuum up any resulting clumps before adding the thinned glue.

Foam clumps to be vacuumed

4-28

To fully define the scenery, add rock debris, shrubs, bushes, taller weeds, and grasses.

Assorted trees

Foliage clusters

Rock debris

STEP 5 Adding a ground foam layer

Covering areas with ground foam to simulate grass, dirt, and weeds follows the same process as making gravel roads (step 3). Start by applying a coat of thick glue to the area you wish to cover, then sprinkle on a base layer of ground foam. I used Woodland Scenics Earth Blend in a shaker bottle, **4-27**. (I've also made my own scenery dispensers by washing out used potato chip cans and drilling ⅛" holes in the top.) Vacuum any excess foam and then follow with the thinned glue from step 4.

While the base layer is soaking, add some additional texture to the scenery by sprinkling different colors and sizes of ground foam onto the wet turf. Because I'm working in N scale, I use only the fine size of foam, but I did sprinkle in some darker green and yellow for variety. Ground foam holds moisture, so make sure you let this scenery layer dry thoroughly for a day before proceeding.

STEP 6 Completing the final layer

In the final layer, I add the rock debris, shrubs, bushes, taller weeds, and grasses that really define the scenery, **4-28**. Woodland Scenics offers a number of different colors of clump- and net-type foliage. The material is easy to work with and can be glued to the scenery with white glue. On most hillsides, I usually pin the clump foliage in place with a T pin until the glue dries.

I've also enjoyed using Scenic Express Prairie Tufts, clumps of static grass that come on a plastic sheet. Simply grab a tuft with a tweezers, dab some white glue on the bottom of the clump, and place it on the layout. They work well for simulating tall grasses that crop up around buildings and along roads. The tufts are flexible enough that you can mount them between railroad ties on industry spurs without fear of causing derailments.

If you're working in larger scales, you may also wish to add bigger grass patches using a static grass applicator, such as the Noch Gras-Master, or Silflor material to simulate taller prairie grasses that grow along roads in fields and fence lines. To finish the scenery, all you need now are some trees, which we'll cover in the next few projects.

PROJECT 4:
Adding simple, realistic trees

Whether it's a fence line along the right-of-way, a small grove next to a farmhouse, or an entire mountain forest, you'll eventually need trees on your layout. Fortunately, manufacturers offer a wide variety of model trees that come ready to use or as kits for scales from Z to G.

Manufactured trees usually have a plastic or wire armature that forms the trunk and branches, though some of the more detailed models use dried plants (see project 5). The armature is covered with poly fiber, ground foam, or both to simulate the foliage found on real trees. Finished trees and tree kits can typically be purchased singly, in small quantities, or in economical bulk packs, making them readily available and affordable. Whenever possible, I use ready-made trees because they are great for quickly filling large spaces, **4-29**.

STEP 1 Shaping

For this project, I used the green deciduous and fall deciduous value-pack trees from Woodland Scenics. These trees come with foam foliage attached to plastic armatures. Even though the trees come ready made, they need a little work before you plant them on the layout.

To save packaging space, the manufacturer presses the trees' foam foliage into tight balls and then instructs the modeler to shape the trees so they don't look like clumps of foam on sticks.

To spread the tree limbs, gently pull apart the foliage canopy, **4-30**. A little of the ground foam will fall off the tree during the shaping process, but don't worry about it – you can use it later to make shrubs and bushes. If too much foliage comes off, you can glue it back on using Woodland Scenics Hob-E-Tac or regular white glue. Once you've finished shaping the trees, you'll notice that some trees look better than others. Save the best-looking ones for foreground trees.

4-29

Using ready-made trees on your layout is an easy way to fill large spaces with realistic greenery.

4-30

When using trees straight from the package, shape them by spreading the branches and gently pulling apart the foliage.

4-31

Once trees are shaped, remove any molding nubs and flash with a sprue cutter.

4-32

To insert a mounting pin in a tree for better support, first drill a hole in the trunk's base with a pin vise and a no. 57 bit.

4-33

Create mounting pins by removing the pinheads with a motor tool and cutoff wheel.

STEP 2 Pruning

After shaping the trees, you'll need to prune them a bit to remove flash, molding nubs, and any unwanted branches. Flash is excess material attached to the plastic casting that's left over from the molding process. A hobby knife and a sprue cutter (a tool made for cutting plastic) are about all you'll need to clean up each tree's plastic armature.

Start by clipping and discarding the plastic base and then remove all visible flash and plastic molding nubs, **4-31**. Once you've finished the shaping and pruning steps, place the trees in flat boxes and sort them by size and color. This aids the tree-selection process and speeds up installation.

STEP 3 Giving new roots

The next step gives trees better roots, steel ones to be exact. I install headless straight pins in the bottom of some trees to provide better support. For larger trees, I use small finishing nails. (Adding mounting pins works only if you are using foam insulation as a scenery base. If not, skip this step.)

This step is not necessary for all trees on a layout, but you'll want to add pins to the trees that will stand by themselves or those that will be near the layout's edges – basically anywhere a tree is likely to take an occasional bump from an operator or visitor. For all other areas of the layout, if you're working with foam scenery, white glue applied to the plastic peg molded on the bottom of the armature is probably enough to keep the tree in place, especially if it's part of a group.

To add a mounting pin, start by clipping the plastic peg from the bottom of the armature. Use a pin vise with a no. 57 bit to drill a ¼"-deep hole into the base of the trunk, **4-32**. Next, remove the head of a straight pin using a motor tool with a cutoff wheel. Be sure to wear the proper eye protection. I clamp the pins in a small vise while cutting, **4-33**.

When you've got enough pins and trees prepared, place a drop of cyanoacrylate adhesive on the headless pin and insert the pin into the hole in the tree trunk. Hold the pin with a pair of pliers as you push it into the trunk.

4-34

For most efficient planting, start at the back and top of a scene, such as the top of a hill, and work your way forward.

4-35

Plant a forest using layered clumps of trees in random sizes and colors.

4-36

Use T pins to keep shrubs in place until the glue dries.

STEP 4 Planting

Planting a tree is easy: select one, dab white glue on its base, and insert its plastic mounting peg into the foam hillside. Trees with steel mounting pins don't need to be glued in place if you want them to remain removable.

Start at the back of a scene, such as the top of the hill, **4-34**, and work your way forward, building the forest in layered clumps. Try to choose sizes and colors that look good together, avoiding predictable patterns, **4-35**. Also, don't be afraid to plant three, four, or even five trees of the same color together – groves of trees grow that way in nature.

STEP 5 Filling in with scrub

Scrub growth (shrubs and young, small trees) typically grows along the edges of tree lines. To simulate this, I used several colors of Woodland Scenics foliage clusters and some leftover tree foliage clumps to fill in the front of the tree line. In addition to adding realism, this step is economical because scrub growth makes your tree line look much bigger than it really is – and you'll use fewer trees in the process.

To add the scrub layer, start by breaking the foliage clusters into small, random clumps. After placing a group of trees on the layout, fill the area directly in front of the trees with the foliage clumps, cementing them in place with white glue. On steep slopes, such as a hillside, you'll need to pin the clumps in place until the glue dries, **4-36**. Again, as with the trees, try not to create predictable size or color patterns.

Once the glue dries (overnight), you can pull out the pins and admire your finished landscape.

STEP 6 Adding shadows (optional)

Unlike model trees, real fall trees never change color all at once but instead have patches of mixed colors. Even green trees appear to be made up of different colors as a result of shadows and sun highlights. You can airbrush highlights and shadows on the foam tree foli-age with water-base paint. (Don't use organic solvent-base paint because it will chemically attack the foam.)

I tried this on some of my trees using several colors of Polly Scale paint. I dusted the tops of the green-colored trees with Reefer Yellow to give them some highlights. On the brightly colored autumn trees, I dulled the foliage a bit by spraying Depot Olive near the bottom, **4-37**.

Painting ground foam foliage is not ideal, and the resulting colors can vary depending on the paint you use. I discovered that some color combinations, like Reefer Yellow on dark green foam, work much better than others. However, when added into a scene, the painted trees looked more realistic than solid-colored ones, **4-38**.

As an alternative, you can spray a tree with diluted matte medium (see project 5) and sprinkle on different colors of fine ground foam. This also varies the colors of the trees and makes them more realistic.

4-37

To dull brightly colored trees, spray them with patches of green paint.

4-38

A mix of painted and solid-colored trees makes for a realistic autumn forest.

4-39

Trees with light, airy branch structures or armatures made from dried plant material have a highly detailed appearance that is perfect for foreground scenes.

PROJECT 5: Modeling foreground trees

Bulk packages of manufactured trees are great for filling large background areas of a layout quickly and economically. However, since modelers tend to put the most detailed scenes in the foreground where people can see them, it only makes sense to surround them with highly detailed trees, **4-39**.

Trees with a light and airy branch structure are especially effective when you take closeup photos of your finished models. On my quest for more realistic trees, I've experimented with a number of different modeling techniques.

One way to get the fine branch detail needed for good model trees is to use dried plants for the armatures. If you're lucky, you may live in a region where suitable model tree material grows in your own backyard. (Western sagebrush is one variety that makes good tree forms.) In that case, simply pick some branches, hang them in your garage for several months until they've completely dried out, and then proceed with the following steps to prepare your trees.

For those of us less fortunate (or patient), however, several manufacturers sell dried plants specifically for making

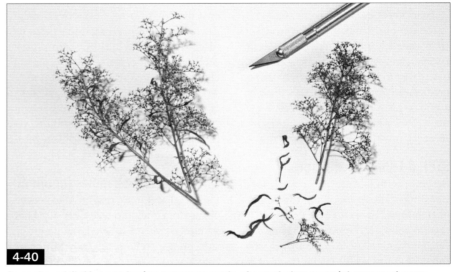

4-40

As packaged (left), trees having armatures made of actual plant material may need some leaves and spare branches removed (right).

model trees. One such product is the Super Tree kit from Scenic Express. With a little practice, using the Super Tree kit is a good way to make an assortment of foreground-worthy trees in a few evenings.

STEP 1 Preparing the branches

For this project, I bought a Super Tree starter kit from Scenic Express. The kit comes with a package of dried plant material for making the armatures, a large assortment of colored ground foam, several plastic trays, a small package of matte medium, a spray bottle, and a set of self-closing tweezers.

The kit includes clear, easy-to-follow instructions, and though they work just fine, I deviated from them a bit to cut down on the mess of trying to spray the trees with matte medium. My own, somewhat neater process is described in the following steps. The N scale tree kit yielded about 60 trees.

To get started, you need to sort, prune, and clean up the natural armatures. The trees come packaged as clusters of branches. At this point in the process, the tree material is brittle, so handle the armatures with care. Some of the branches may be just right for trees, but most will need some trimming. A sprue nipper works well for this job.

Once you have the armatures shaped, you'll need to remove the few remaining leaves. A small, sharp hobby knife is well suited for this task, **4-40**.

STEP 2 Soaking the armatures

The next step is to soak the armatures in diluted matte medium (one part matte medium to seven parts water). The dried branches used as trees will eventually disintegrate unless they're sealed in some way. The matte medium preserves the armature's cellular structure and also makes it somewhat flexible. This means if you bump the tree after it's been installed on your layout, it should give a little and not simply snap off. Be sure you use matte medium for this step. Unlike white glue, matte medium stays flexible and dries flat and clear.

To soak the trees, you'll need more matte medium than comes in the Super Tree kit. You can find it at any store that sells art supplies. I used an old one-quart container for the soaking step, **4-41**. A container with a snap-on lid lets you save the soaking solution for making more trees later.

Once you've diluted the matte medium, simply dunk the branches into it. Let them soak for 30 to 60 seconds, then remove the branches and clip them to a drying line. To straighten bent trunks, clip a tweezers or clothes pin to the top of the branch and let gravity do the rest, **4-42**.

The matte medium dries quickly, so unless it's exceptionally humid, your armatures should be ready for the next step in a few hours. Drying the armatures outdoors speeds up the process.

STEP 3 Painting the tree trunks

According to Super Tree instructions, you can paint the trunks at any time in the process. However, it seemed better to paint them after they'd been preserved, ensuring that the bare armatures would soak up as much matte medium as possible.

You can use just about any type of paint, including the acrylic spray paints used by florists. I airbrushed my armatures with acrylic model paints. Since

Soaking dried branches in a solution of one part matte medium to seven parts water helps preserve them and make them more flexible.

Weighting trees with tweezers or clothes pins as they hang on the drying line will straighten crooked trunks.

Light gray for maple trees

Dark gray for oak and hickory trees

Spraying bare armatures with shades of gray paint helps simulate the trunks of different tree species.

Yellow sprinkled on top

Light green sprinkled on lower half of tree

4-44

After dipping the top of the armature in matte medium, apply the foam foliage, using a tweezers to hold the tree. *Bill Zuback*

4-45

To finish trees for planting, apply a second layer of foam leaves, if necessary, and hang trees out to dry.

the tree trunks are very light, you'll need to clamp them down so they stay put while spraying. Clothespins make good tree holders and also provide a convenient handle for holding the trunk while painting it.

If you look closely, you'll see that most tree trunks aren't actually brown but some shade of gray, depending upon the species. I sprayed some armatures with Polly Scale Union Pacific Dark Gray to represent oak and hickory trees; I also sprayed some with UP Harbor Mist Gray to be maples, **4-43**.

I tried spraying a few white to look like birch trees, but the branches' greenish color gave the paint a light gray-green tint. I have subsequently

gotten better results by brush-painting those trunks with a thicker coat of white paint. I then used a little black paint to make the characteristic birch-bark markings.

Keep the painted armatures from touching each other until the paint is completely dry. Otherwise the branches tend to stick, making it difficult to separate them without damaging the armature.

STEP 4 Adding foliage and planting

Adding foliage to the armatures is fun because they look like trees when you've finished. The Super Trees kit comes with a nice assortment of colored ground foam and includes some

pleasant fall colors, which is great for me since I'm modeling trees during early October.

Although the instructions call for spraying the trees with matte medium in this step (a messy prospect at best), a neater choice is to dip them in the stuff.

To apply the foliage, start by dunking the treetop into the diluted mixture of matte medium, which acts as an adhesive. Next, hold the tree upright over one of the kit's plastic trays, sprinkle your choice of ground foam on top of the tree, and then gently shake off any excess material, **4-44**. The ground-foam leaves look best if they're added from the top of the tree, leaving a lot of branch detail visible from below.

If one application doesn't put enough leaves on the branches, quickly dip part or all of the tree back in the matte medium and repeat the process. Though this may wash off some of the first layer of ground foam, most of it will remain.

When you're happy with the end result, hang the finished tree on the drying line, **4-45**.

Once the trees are dry, they're ready to plant on the layout. Drill a small hole in the scenery, add a dab of white glue to the bottom of the trunk, and slip the tree into place, **4-46**.

4-46

To plant a tree in the foreground, first make a hole in the scenery with a T pin, add some white glue to the trunk, and then carefully place the tree in the hole with a tweezers.

4-47

Having needles instead of leaves, conifers add a nice contrast to deciduous trees in a mixed forest.

PROJECT 6:
Creating conifers

Although I'm modeling Connecticut in the fall, up to this point, I've used only deciduous trees on my layout. However, to be true to the region, I also needed some conifers – more universally referred to as pine trees or evergreens since they stay green all year, **4-47**.

While ready-made trees can cover a lot of ground in a hurry, they're also often the most expensive option. Building trees from kits can save money.

One manufacturer that offers nice conifer tree kits is Sweetwater Scenery. These kits include stained wood trunks, poly fiber material for the branches, and ground-foam foliage representing the needles. The kits come in an assortment of sizes, they are easy to build, and no two trees end up looking exactly the same.

STEP 1 Forming branches

The trunks in the Sweetwater kit come stained a light brown color, but I wanted them to be darker, so I gave them a thin wash of black paint diluted in rubbing

alcohol. This darkened the trunks substantially, and since the alcohol evaporates quickly, this extra step did not slow down my tree production very much.

While the trunks dried, I began making the branches. Start by cutting the poly fiber pad into small squares using a pair of scissors. This material is made up of about four interwoven layers and needs to be pulled apart, **4-48**. Once the pad is separated, pull smaller tufts from the layers and fluff them out a bit. These form the tree branches.

The poly fiber branches slip onto the carved wood trunk. I placed a drop of

4-48

To shape conifer branches, pull apart the poly fiber squares and then tuft the pieces to give them an airy appearance. *Bill Zuback*

4-49

Slip the tufts onto the wooden trunk off center and stagger them to create a more natural pattern. *Bill Zuback*

4-50

Trim any wild edges and tufted strands between branches to give the tree a realistic shape. *Bill Zuback*

white glue at the base to hold the first layer of branches in place; the others can simply slide down on top of them. Slip the tufts onto the trunk slightly off-center and stagger them to give some variation to the branches, 4-49. When you get to the top of the tree, place another drop of white glue on the point of the trunk to hold the uppermost tuft.

On my first batch of trees, I used too many poly fiber branches, making my trees look too dense, 4-52. On later trees, I used fewer branches, giving the finished trees a more realistic open structure and airy appearance.

STEP 2 Trimming

After you've attached the branches to several trees, you need to shape and trim them. To shape the branches, simply slide them around on the trunk, positioning them so they look natural. You can also pull the poly fiber apart as needed to fill in bare areas.

Once you're satisfied with the branch location, it's time to trim the tree. Using a pair of scissors, clip away any long stray fiber strands to make the tree look more pine-like, 4-50. Next, add definition to the layers of branches by clipping away some of the tufted strands between the branches. This not only opens up the tree, it helps accent the distinct branch structure characteristic of pine trees.

STEP 3 Adding needles

The final step in the project is adding ground-foam needles to the trees. The instructions in the kit suggest using hair spray for an adhesive, which will work just fine, but I used diluted matte medium (one part matte medium to seven parts water), since that's what I used for project 5. The mounting pin in the bottom of the trunk makes the trees easy to hold during this step.

If you dunk the trees directly into the diluted matte medium, the poly fiber branches soak up too much liquid, causing them to sag and make something of a mess. (Yes, I found this out the hard way.) Instead, I poured the diluted matte medium into a misting bottle and sprayed the tree branches over a plastic-lined garbage can – a much neater solution. You want the poly fiber to be wet but not soaked with matte medium.

Next, sprinkle the ground foam onto the tree, making sure to work it into the spaces between the branches. I applied the ground foam to the tree over an old kit box, 4-51. This way the excess foam is easy to collect and reuse for the next batch of trees.

After applying the foam, I stuck the trees into a foam insulation block to let them dry overnight, 4-52. The next day, I planted the trees on the layout.

4-51
To give a pine tree needles, spray it with hair spray or diluted matte medium and sprinkle ground foam on the branches. *Bill Zuback*

4-52
Stick the finished trees in a foam block and let them dry overnight before planting them on your layout. *Bill Zuback*

PROJECT 7: Crafting cool water

Water is one of the most impressive scenery elements on any model railroad. For years, modelers have used a variety of techniques to produce rivers, streams, and ponds that have depth and waves. These water-crafting methods often involved delicately cutting and shaping pieces of rippled glass or using highly unpleasant smelling casting resins.

Fortunately, thanks to some recent products, making dramatic water effects on your layout is now easier than ever, 4-53. And best of all, these new materials produce great results while being nearly odorless and easy to clean up with water.

STEP 1 Making riverbeds and banks

Like many other scenery projects, creating realistic water is accomplished by applying scenic materials in layers. To make rivers, ponds, and other water bodies, you need to start at the bottom and work your way up. I made my riverbed directly on the wood surface of the hollow-core door that forms the base of my layout, 4-54, but plywood also makes a good riverbed. The water's base must be smooth and sturdy – trying to build water features on flexible materials does not work well since they can warp or crack.

The main river on my layout is a representation of the Naugatuck River in Connecticut. It's prone to flooding, so it has a lot of riprap (rock debris) piled along the shores to prevent erosion. To make the riprap, I mixed two sizes of Woodland Scenics talus and some silica sand in a small container and then glued it to the banks using the two-part adhesive described in project 3. I let the banks dry for several days and then vacuumed up any loose material.

This is also the right time to finish all surrounding scenery that requires thinned liquid glue. Once the river is installed, this type of glue can seep under the water layer and ruin it.

Kit box that collects excess foam

STEP 2 Preparing the riverbed

I prepared the riverbed by scraping away any errant scenery materials and checking that the wood surface was clean and smooth.

Because high-grade plywood is smooth to the touch, it's very tempting to begin the painting step and speed up the process. Don't do it! Wood surfaces are deceptive, and wood grain can show through multiple coats of paint. (Trust me, you don't want a wood-grain river.) Fill the grain using a good quality spackling compound. Don't use joint compound because it contains too much water and may raise the grain or warp the wood.

Start by applying a thin layer of spackling with your fingers, **4-55**, and work it over the entire surface. Then scrape away all the spackling you can with a sharp putty knife. You may find that you end up removing most of the spackling from the surface, **4-56**. This is a good thing because if the spackling is applied too thick, it can crack or flake away later.

STEP 3 Painting the depths

The easiest way to create the illusion of depth is with paint. Water bodies, unless they are very muddy, appear dark when viewed from above; however, they are lighter at the edges and where the water is shallow. To create this effect, I painted the bottom of the river black, using a fast-drying latex paint, **4-57**. Because a little black paint goes a long way, I used Rust-Oleum semi-gloss black latex paint, which is available in half-pint containers.

I applied the paint with a 1" soft-bristle brush in one even coat. Don't worry about getting the paint too close to the edges – you'll paint those a different color later. Painting within ¼" of the shore is close enough. The Rust-Oleum dries quickly, so you can airbrush the banks in the same evening.

STEP 4 Painting the banks

To complete the illusion of depth, feather the shore color out into the black center, so it appears that the riverbed slopes down and away from the bank. The easiest way to achieve this illusion is to airbrush the river's banks with a lighter color – usually one that

4-53

With new materials, such as Realistic Water and Water Effects, making impressive water features is easily achieved.

Modeling tips for water

- **Finish all base scenery work first, so liquid adhesives can't seep under the water layer and damage it.**

- **Fill and sand smooth all wood surfaces before applying water materials. This prevents the wood grain from showing through the finished river.**

- **Airbrush the banks in multiple coats. By building up the paint slowly, you make a smoother feathered edge and create a more convincing illusion of depth. Make sure all paints are completely dry before pouring the water layer.**

- **Pour a minimum of two layers of water material, such as Realistic Water, and don't make any single layer thicker than ⅛". Wash all tools immediately after use.**

- **Always pour water material into the center of the stream or pond to prevent high-water marks as the material seeks its own level.**

- **Keep tools, models, and other objects off the finished water to avoid marring its surface. To make repairs, dab more water material over any damaged areas with a paintbrush.**

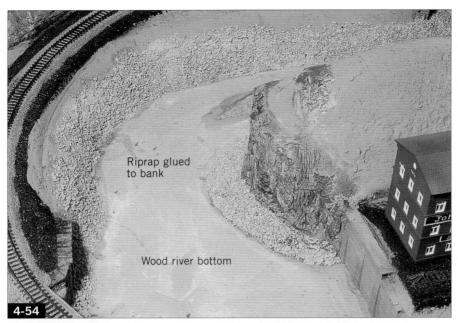

Riprap glued
to bank

Wood river bottom

4-54

Before pouring the river, it is a good idea to finish any surrounding scenery so that the scenery cement doesn't seep under the water layer.

matches your scenery's ground color. I chose Polly Scale Mud for my banks as it looked close to the colors of the ground cover and the riprap on the shore.

I applied paint in three coats. On the first pass, I painted the river's edge where the riprap meets the black river bottom. For the second coat, I painted the same shore area but feathered the paint deeper into the black, **4-58**. Feathering is the misty effect created along the edge of the spray pattern that allows most of the base coat to show through. I also started to fill in several areas where sandbars would logically develop, such as at the base of the bridge piers and off the rocky point. On the final coat, I filled in the centers of the sandbars. The best part about working with paints is that if you mess up, you can simply break out the black paint and start over.

4-55

Exposed wood grain can show through water layers, so cover it with a layer of quick-drying spackling.

4-56

Scraping away excess wet spackling with a sharp putty knife provides a smooth surface for creating your river.

4-57

To produce a feeling of depth, paint the river bottom black, keeping away from the banks where the water is lighter and shallower.

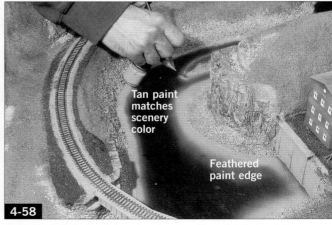

Tan paint
matches
scenery
color

Feathered
paint edge

4-58

By feathering the bank in several coats of a paint that matches your scenery's ground color, you avoid a sharp edge between colors and complete the illusion of depth.

If you wish to add objects like old tires, tin cans, or rocks in the shallower parts of the river, now is the time to glue them in place.

STEP 5 Pouring water

Pouring the river is the easiest part of the project. I used Woodland Scenics Realistic Water. It's a low-odor resin that requires no mixing, stays flexible, and cleans up with water. The material is thin enough so that it's self-leveling but thick enough that it can be easily contained with masking-tape dams at each end of the river. Make sure your river surface is level before you pour the water, or you'll wind up with all of it at one end.

Pour each layer of water into the center of the river, 4-59. Avoid pouring the resin next to the shore, bridge piers, or retaining walls – the resin will leave a wet-looking high-water mark on these objects that you won't be able to remove. Instead, use a soft art brush to work the resin out to the edges, creating a wet path for the water material to follow as it seeks its own level, 4-60.

You can apply as many coats as you wish, ⅛" thick at a time. My river is two layers thick. Allow 24 hours of drying time between each layer.

STEP 6 Making waves

After the water layers have set for several days, add the waves. As a companion product to its Realistic Water, Woodland Scenics offers Water Effects for making waves, rapids, and waterfalls. This paste-like product comes in a squeeze bottle, and while it looks like white glue when first applied, it dries to a clear finish.

To make waves, simply dab a small puddle of the material on the river surface and then use a paintbrush to move it around, forming waves or rapids. If you want to model higher waves or faster rapids, apply additional coats in those areas as I did for the center of the river, 4-61. You can also highlight the tips with water-base white paint to simulate whitecaps or foam.

While adding the waves, this is a good time to place finishing details like boats, swimmers, and anglers, 4-62. The Water Effects material will hold them in place and make them look like they are floating in the water.

4-59

Pour the Realistic Water in the center of the river and work it into the edges. The material will appear hazy until it dries.

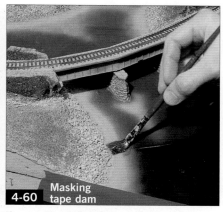

4-60 Masking tape dam

Use a soft paintbrush to work the resin from the center to the edges, giving the material a path to follow.

4-61

Squeeze wave material onto your river surface and form waves with a paintbrush.

4-62

Before the waves dry, add details like boats, so they look like they are floating in the water.

5-1

CHAPTER FIVE

Building structures

The *River Job*, the local train that works the industries along the Naugatuck River, passes the Waterbury Gas Works and American Brass. These important industries on the layout started as ordinary plastic kits, then were cut up and reassembled to fit their purpose and location.

Just like scenery, trackwork, and even the trains themselves, structures play an important part in building a realistic model railroad. The buildings you select for your layout can provide a corporate identity for your railroad, such as using a common style of station or other lineside buildings. Your structures also define the types of industries your railroad serves, **5-1**. For example, one would expect to see hopper cars or tank cars spotted at a fuel dealer. And the buildings you choose also say a lot about the types of communities your railroad connects. An urban scene indicates a much different type of railroad operation than a quiet prairie town does.

Fortunately for modelers, there's an amazing selection of structure kits available for N, HO, and O scales. These kits come in a variety of materials, including plastic, wood, etched brass, cast resin, and plaster. The projects in this chapter describe techniques for working with wood and plastic kits, and project 3 in chapter 6 uses a resin structure kit.

5-2

Self-adhesive doors, windows, trim, and other pieces give laser-cut wood structure kits a highly detailed appearance.

PROJECT 1:
Building a wood structure kit

Modern, laser-cut wood structure kits are some of the best-kept secrets in model railroading. Because wood kits have been a part of the hobby since the beginning, many modelers overlook these newer wood kits as being outdated, lacking detail, or requiring a high level of skill. Actually, most of the laser-cut wood kits on the market are highly detailed structures and require no more skill to assemble than most injection-molded styrene kits, 5-2.

For this project, I used a Dill's Market kit from American Model Builders (available in N, HO, and O scales). The kit contains an assortment of laser-cut wood sheets that include the walls, roof, and self-adhesive details such as windows, doors, and trim. The kit also comes with an instruction sheet, window glazing, and a cast-metal chimney.

Before doing anything else, look over the instructions so you can easily identify the parts. Unlike a plastic kit, wood kits don't have sprue numbers for individual pieces, so it's important to know what you have before starting to cut out parts.

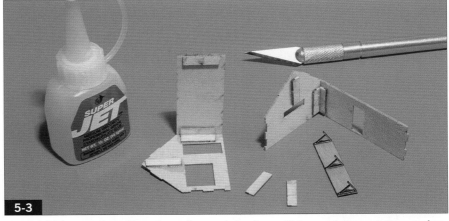

5-3

You should support the wall sections of a wood structure with braces to prevent any warping or sagging that results from painting.

STEP 1 Cutting and bracing

Although the instructions suggest painting the parts before cutting them out, I prefer assembling and bracing the walls and roof first to minimize warping. The laser cuts on the pieces are nearly complete, leaving only small tabs holding the parts in place on the sheet. To free the parts, cut the tabs using a hobby knife with a fresh, sharp blade. Cutting the pieces on a self-healing mat, which supports the material, helps prevent the pieces from breaking. It also keeps knife blades sharp. After cutting out the parts, I test-fit them. I use a sanding stick to smooth any remaining tabs.

You can use a variety of adhesives to assemble laser-cut models but beware of those with a high water content, such as white glue, because they cause parts to warp. I prefer gap-filling cyanoacrylate adhesive as it cements parts together quickly and securely without warping the wood.

It's a good idea to brace the wall sections when building a wood kit, 5-3. Because the wood has been milled with siding patterns, the wall pieces are rigid running with the grain but somewhat flexible across the grain. If you don't add bracing across the grain, the parts will warp or sag when you paint them.

Making a solid joint where the walls and subroof meet further stabilizes the building.

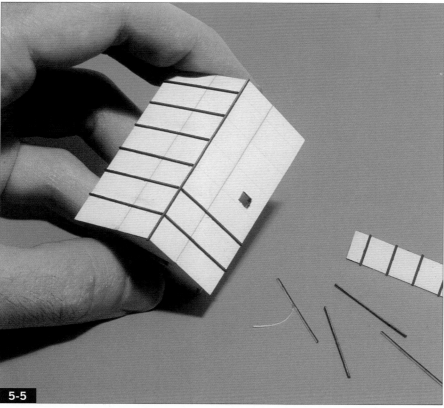

Applying sheets of peel-and-stick paper and strips of self-adhesive wood battens puts a tar-paper roof on the lumberyard's office.

I made simple braces from the remaining scraps of the kit's wood. I also added interior corner braces to keep the building square.

STEP 2 Putting a roof overhead

Putting a roof on Dill's Market started with the wood subroof. Because this kit has no base and is accessible from the bottom, I attached the subroof to stabilize the walls. I also added bracing to form a solid joint where the subroof meets the walls, **5-4**.

Once the subroof was in place, I applied the peel-and-stick paper layer and the thin, self-adhesive wood battens, **5-5**. This arrangement represents a tar-paper roof; however, for a different look, you could use other materials such as paper or styrene shingles or corrugated-metal roofing.

At this point, I also assembled the front awning but didn't attach it until later to make painting easier.

STEP 3 Painting the model

After spraying the structure and its parts with Rust-Oleum Light Gray Primer to seal the wood, I used Polly Scale paints on my model. I started by brush-painting the walls with two light coats of Depot Buff and the roof with UP Harbor Mist Gray.

Doors, windows, and trim are easier to paint while still attached to their wood sheet, **5-6**. These parts have a self-adhesive backing, so you need to paint only one side. (Be careful if you use a solvent-base paint like Floquil – applying too much paint will dissolve the adhesive.) To avoid plugging the delicate details of the windows, I applied the paint with my airbrush. I sprayed the parts Polly Scale U. S. Tactical Medium Green (no. 505390 in its military line), making a good contrast to the wall paint.

STEP 4 Adding doors and windows

Doors, windows, and other details are fairly easy to add after painting as long as there is still an opening in either the bottom or the top of the structure. In fact, most laser-cut wood kits have you build doors, windows, and trim details using multiple layers of self-adhesive parts, making it easier to create fancy painting effects.

I used this assembly technique when I built the front and side doors. I wanted the doors to have a two-tone paint scheme, so I left the frame and raised door detail layer the same color as the windows but painted the door slabs Depot Buff. When assembling the pieces, I had neatly finished doors, **5-7**.

The doors and windows fit easily in the wall openings and are held in place by the self-adhesive trim.

STEP 5 Completing assembly

Completing the model includes installing the trim boards and chimney. The trim boards are self-adhesive and simply stick in place. After completing the trim, I cemented the awning to the front of the building with CA, **5-8**.

The chimney is a solid metal casting. To improve its appearance, I drilled a hole through the chimney cap using a no. 61 bit in a pin vise, **5-9**. The chimney slips through a hole in the roof, and since it is much longer than need be, I secured it by cementing the bottom to the inside wall with CA. I painted the chimney Polly Scale Boxcar Red and the cap Depot Buff.

Before moving the building to the layout, I weathered it by airbrushing a light dusting of L&N Gray around the base and on the edges of the roof to simulate dust left on those surfaces by rain. I also airbrushed Engine Black around the top and base of the chimney to represent soot deposits.

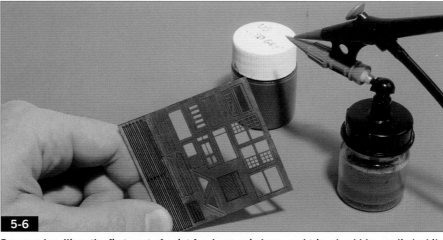

For easy handling, the first coat of paint for doors, windows, and trim should be applied while the pieces are still attached to the trim sheet.

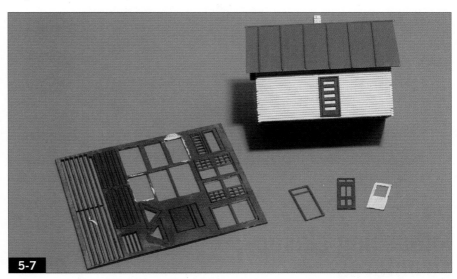

A detailed-looking painting scheme is not difficult to achieve when using multiple layers of self-adhesive parts.

Final assembly of the wood structure includes painting the chimney, installing trim boards, and adding the awning.

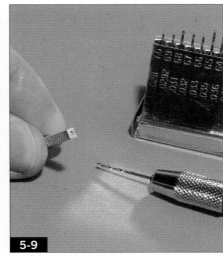

Drilling a shallow hole in the cap of the cast-metal chimney with a pin vise and no. 61 bit (.039) provides a more realistic look.

5-10

The Hanson Piano Co. plant had to be kitbashed in order to fit in the tight, wedge-shaped space between the tracks and a hill.

PROJECT 2:
Kitbashing plastic structures

With the amazing number of structure kits available to model railroaders, chances are good that you can find the buildings you want for the factories, businesses, and homes on your layout. If you can't, it's fairly easy to modify existing kits (called kitbashing) to make the structures you need. The following example shows how I kitbashed a structure to fit a wedge-shaped space on my layout, **5-10**. You can use these techniques to make unique structures for your own model railroad.

STEP 1 Survey the site

To build the Hanson Piano Co. plant, I started with a Design Preservation Models (DPM) N scale Gripp's Luggage kit (no. 506). If you're working in HO scale, you could build a similar structure by combining parts

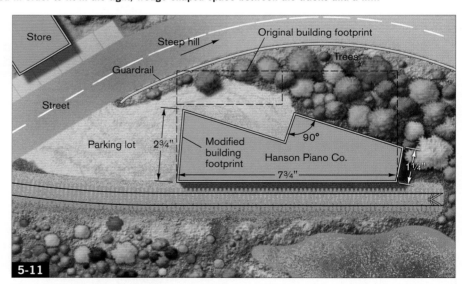

5-11

The dashed line indicates the space needed for the DPM kit, and the modified footprint shows how the building was altered to fit. *Illustration by Rick Johnson*

from two DPM Laube's Linen Mill kits (no. 106). The DPM kit includes six plastic walls with all door and window details molded in place, a sheet of styrene for the roof, and two styrene tubes for making the twin smokestacks. The kit is ideal for customizing projects because you can easily cut apart the walls with a razor saw and reassemble them in new ways.

The space on my layout where I wanted to place the Hanson Piano factory did not work, **5-11**. The DPM kit was obviously too big. By altering

5-12

Marking the discarded portion of the original wall with a piece of tape eliminates any cutting mistakes.

the finished shape of the kit and raising the ground on the street side so it would be level with the loading dock, I was able to make enough room for the structure without unrealistically crowding the corner.

To get a feel for how the finished building will fit on the layout, temporarily hold the walls together with masking tape. This way, you can experiment with possible changes before cutting any parts.

STEP 2 Cleaning and cutting walls

The DPM kit pieces have large tabs on them left over from the molding process. Use a sprue nipper or sharp hobby knife to carefully remove the molding tabs. After cleaning the walls, file or sand the edges smooth.

By cutting just one wall and changing the angles of several corners, you can make a wedge-shaped building from the original, **5-12**.

Use a razor saw for this step. Place the saw blade along the brick pilaster, which makes a good guide for a

Modeling tools

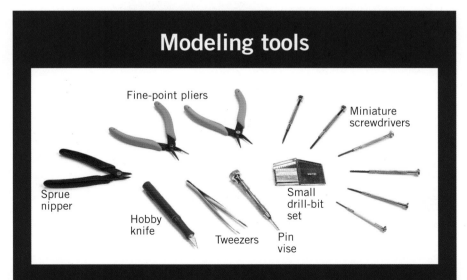

Fine-point pliers

Miniature screwdrivers

Sprue nipper

Hobby knife

Tweezers

Pin vise

Small drill-bit set

I use this group of tools for most modeling work. In addition to the basic tools like hobby knives, pin vises, and miniature screwdrivers, I also have two pairs of fine-point jeweler's pliers. They look similar to each other but are actually different: one has a smooth jaw while the other is serrated for gripping objects better. I use both types of pliers and the tweezers to place details.

The sprue nippers, like rail nippers, are a specialized cutter. The blades are very sharp and work great for quickly trimming plastic parts such as tree trunks or railroad ties. Sanding sticks (not shown) are small abrasive tools that are useful for smoothing cut edges or for making fine adjustments to parts so they fit tightly.

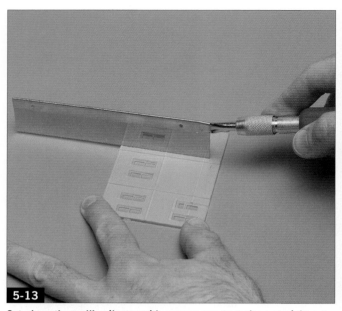

5-13

Cut along the wall's pilaster with a razor saw to make a straight cut.

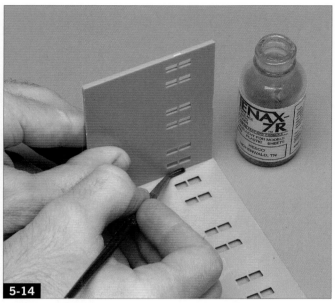

5-14

Apply liquid plastic cement to the joints with a small, natural bristle paintbrush.

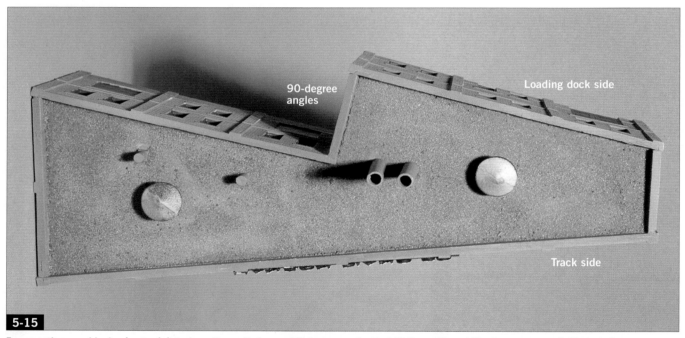

5-15

90-degree angles

Loading dock side

Track side

For smooth assembly, begin at a joint where the walls form a 90-degree angle. Test-fit the walls and file the corners to fit if needed.

straight cut. Make gentle cuts until the saw blade works its way through the plastic. Then after cutting, file the new edge smooth.

STEP 3 Assembling walls

It's easiest to begin assembling the structure at any joint where the walls form a 90-degree corner, **5-15**. Test-fit the pieces before cementing them together, making any necessary corrections with a small file.

Glue the walls with liquid plastic cement, using a small paintbrush to apply the cement, **5-14**. Hold two wall sections together and run a bead of cement along the seam, letting the liquid wick into the joint. After only a few seconds, the plastic walls will bond and you can let go. Use a small square to make sure the corner fits correctly. If you need to make any adjustments, do so immediately. It doesn't take long for the joint to set

hard, making it impossible to change how the walls are aligned without cutting them apart.

For the remaining walls that don't form square corners, use a file or sanding stick to shape the edges so the outer surface joints are flush. When you are sure you have a tight fit, cement the walls together with liquid plastic cement. Let the glued joints dry thoroughly before handling the model.

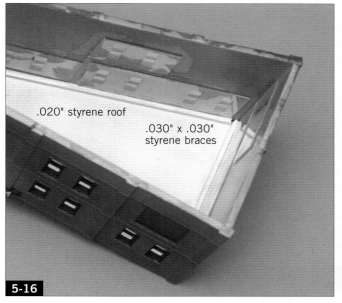

5-16

Placing styrene braces around the building's interior perimeter adds a stable base when attaching the roof.

.020" styrene roof

.030" x .030" styrene braces

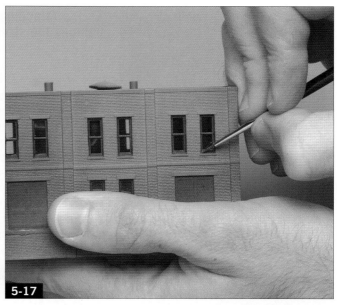

5-17

Use a fine paintbrush to paint trim such as doors and windows.

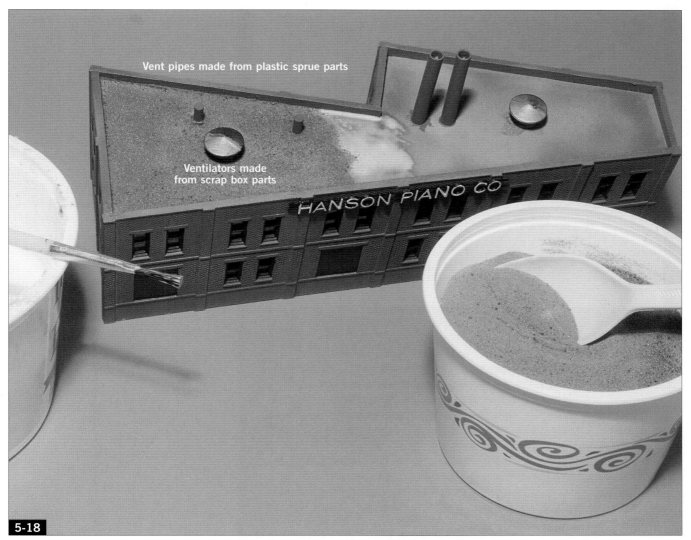

5-18

Vent pipes made from plastic sprue parts

Ventilators made from scrap box parts

HANSON PIANO CO

To create a gravel roof, brush on white glue diluted 20 percent with water and sprinkle on fine ballast.

.010" clear
styrene sheet

5-19

Painting the backs of some clear styrene windows with tan paint adds window shades to the building.

STEP 4 Attaching the roof and painting the structure

The roof for the DPM kit is made from .020" styrene sheet. To fit the roof, trace the inside walls of the building onto the styrene with a mechanical pencil. Cut the roof out of the sheet using a sharp hobby knife and a metal straightedge. Test-fit the roof and make any necessary adjustments with a file.

To support the roof, cement .030"-square styrene strips around the perimeter ⅛" from the top of the wall, **5-16**. Attach the roof by dropping it inside the walls and gluing it to the supports with liquid plastic cement.

I painted the brick walls Polly Scale D&RGW Building Brown and the doors and windows Roof Brown.

Painting the doors and windows is the most delicate step of the project, but it also produces the most dramatic results, **5-17**. The nice part is that if you make a mistake while painting the trim, you can touch it up simply by painting over your error with more of the wall color.

I painted the smokestacks Union Pacific Dark Gray and weathered their tops with black to represent built-up soot.

STEP 5 Detailing the roof

Since model railroaders spend a lot of time viewing models from above, add some details to the roof to improve the building's appearance. To finish the roof, start by cementing the smokestacks and other rooftop details in place. I included several ventilators left over from an old Model Power kit and some vent pipes made from pieces of plastic sprue material. Other good industrial roof details include piping, tanks, air conditioners, access hatches, ladders, and stairways.

To simulate a gravel roof, I used Highball Products no. 125 N scale brown ballast. To apply the ballast to the roof, mix four parts white glue and one part water in a separate container. Working in small sections, brush a thin layer of diluted glue on the roof's surface, carefully working around rooftop details, **5-18**. Next, sprinkle the ballast on top of the glue and let it sit for about 20 to 30 seconds before dumping off the remaining ballast in a box or bin for reuse. Let the gravel roof dry overnight.

STEP 6 Adding final details

With the roof complete, it's time to add the final details. The kit comes with a sheet of .010" clear styrene to be used for window glaze. Cut the styrene to size and cement it in place.

To simulate window shades, paint the back of some of the clear-styrene windows cream or tan, **5-19**. (I also used this technique on many of the buildings shown in chapter 6.) Viewed from the exterior of the building, the paint looks like a window shade. If

More modeling tools

Gravity cup

Airbrush

Motor tool

Spray tips

Paint bottles

Air regulator

Assorted motor tool bits

Cutoff disks

Beyond the basic set of layout construction tools, there are several additional tools you may wish to eventually own.

An airbrush is an incredibly useful modeling tool. I've used mine to paint roads, track, river bottoms, and rock formations and to weather just about everything on the layout. There is a wide variety of airbrushes on the market with something available to fit most everyone's budget. You don't need a big, industrial-size air compressor either. A number of manufacturers offer small, quiet hobby compressors that give good results.

A motor tool is another versatile modeling device and a good addition to any workshop. Thanks to a host of interchangeable bits, a motor tool can function as a grinder, buffer, cutter, router, sander, or drill and has a number of other uses depending upon the accessories. I use mine for cutting gaps in rails to create electrical blocks, for cleaning switch points after ballasting, and for a host of other tasks.

5-20

Making a company's sign with plastic letters gives it a 3-D effect for more prominence.

5-21

Inserting a strip of black cardboard as a view block keeps visitors and operators from looking into an empty building.

your shades contain brush marks or appear streaky, simply apply a second coat of paint.

I made the large sign for the track side of the building using 6mm plastic letters from Slater's Plastikard Ltd., an English company, **5-20**. Cement the letters to two .015" x .020" strips and then paint the whole sign black, letters and all. The letters have a flat face, making them easy to paint. (I painted mine an off-white, so they'd stand out

against the black.) When the paint has dried, attach the finished sign to the building with CA.

Finally, to keep visitors from seeing through the empty model, add a view block. I cut mine from a strip of black cardboard and inserted it into the building, **5-21**.

With that, the piano factory is ready to take its place on the layout and begin adding musical carloads of commerce to the railroad.

PROJECT 3: Using modular structure kits

The space available on a layout for structures, particularly lineside industries served by your railroads, can vary widely. The universal constant with layout space, however, is that there never seems to be quite enough. When faced

5-22

The pin company on my layout was constructed of modular plastic and wood wall sections.

5-23

Set modular wall pieces in place to mark the building's footprint on your layout.

Loading door locations

5-24

Once the foundation of the warehouse was positioned on the layout, I marked the loading door locations for use with 40-foot boxcars.

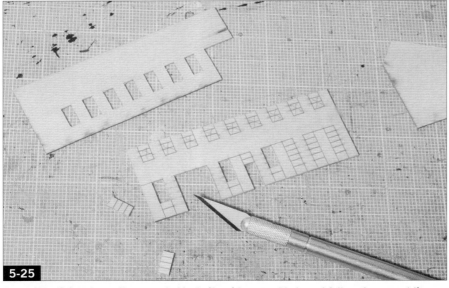

5-25

To avoid splitting the walls, use a hobby knife with a new blade and follow the scored lines on the window and door openings.

with a location where stock structure kits just won't do, your choices are usually limited to kitbashing or scratchbuilding. However, depending upon the type of building you're looking for, you may be able to use one or more modular structure kits to solve the problem, **5-22**.

Because they're hybrids, modular structure kits offer the flexibility of kitbashing and scratchbuilding as well as the simplicity of building off-the-shelf models. Modular kits are available in a variety of architectural styles and typically have either wood or plastic parts. With modular structure components, you can easily arrange them to fit unusual spaces. Want to make a larger building? Simply add more walls or tack on a different modular kit to give your industry a corporate expansion look.

STEP 1 Establishing footprints and foundations

I needed an industry that would fit into a long, narrow location sandwiched between the tracks and a road on my layout. As if that weren't enough of a challenge, the structure also had to be angled to accommodate a riverbank and nestle around a freestanding backdrop.

Because the industry would actually wrap around the backdrop and run along one side of it, I used two different structures – a brick main factory building along the river and a wood-frame warehouse that fit flush along the backdrop. To make the brick factory, I used an assortment of plastic DPM modular brick wall sections. For the warehouse, I selected a Bar Mills laser-cut wood 1-Kit.

Before assembling anything, however, I established the footprint for each building to get an idea of how it would fit on the layout. First, I temporarily taped the DPM wall sections together to position them on the layout, **5-23**. When I was satisfied with the building and its location, I marked the final footprint on the layout with a pencil. I repeated the exercise to mark the warehouse footprint, this time using wall sections from the Bar Mills kit.

To look correct, my wood-frame warehouse needed some type of foundation. I built one from .040" styrene sheet to match the warehouse's footprint and faced the styrene foundation walls with strips of Kibri no. 7960 plastic stone sheet. I then set the foundation in position on the layout and marked the loading door locations, **5-24**.

STEP 2 Constructing a warehouse

The Bar Mills 1-Kit includes four blank walls that have wood siding detail on the front and are laser-etched on the back for standard placement of doors and windows. The kit also includes several sheets of laser-cut windows, trim, and an assortment of different entry and freight doors.

After figuring the wall requirements (step 1), I marked the window and door openings and set to work cutting them out, **5-25**. Even though the openings are partially scored, it took quite a bit of gentle cutting with a sharp knife to avoid splitting the part. I used several new hobby knife blades to make the 37 window and door openings on my warehouse.

Next, I attached the walls to the foundation and braced the walls and corners with stripwood, **5-26**. I used Jet medium-viscosity CA, which works well for bonding wood to plastic. To brace the seams, I cemented a small slip of paper over the area, **5-27**.

The kit includes a sheet of 10-pane windows, but if you want smaller ones as I did, you'll need to cut them to size. I used eight-pane and four-pane windows on my structure and found it worked best to assemble the window and its trim piece before cementing it into the opening. Once this assembly was in place, I added the window sill.

The 1-Kit doesn't include a roof, so I made one from a section of Kibri no. 7967 plastic shingle sheet. I cemented it in place with CA and braced the edges with pieces of stripwood. I also made a narrow loading dock (step 5) from scrap styrene.

STEP 3 Assembling the factory

For the factory portion of the pin company, I used an assortment of one- and two-story wall sections from DPM.

Cement the wooden walls to the plastic foundation with gap-filling CA.

For additional strength, support wall splices with paper and brace the corners with stripwood.

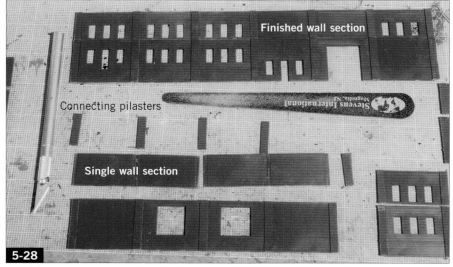
After filing for a proper fit, cement pilasters at seams to join wall sections.

5-29

Sanding with a medium-grit stick may be needed to square plastic wall corners and to ensure a good fit.

5-30

After applying dry transfer letters to the factory, powdered pastels can be used to weather the sign.

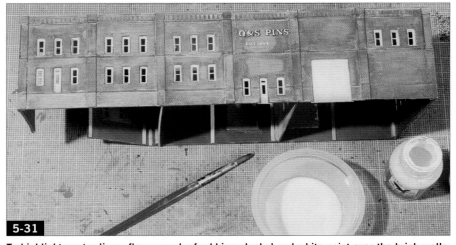

5-31

To highlight mortar lines, flow a wash of rubbing alcohol and white paint over the brick walls. Before the wash dries, remove the white from the surface areas of the walls.

Unlike the 1-Kit, the DPM wall sections have the door and window openings molded in place, so you don't have to cut them out yourself.

The plastic brick wall sections are molded in pairs but are easy to cut apart with a hobby knife or razor saw. I used an assortment of single and double wall pieces to make my factory, **5-28**. The walls are joined at the seams using connecting pilasters, which require filing for proper fit. I bonded the pilasters in place with liquid plastic cement and then reinforced the joints from the back of the wall with scrap pieces of .020" styrene strips.

The wall sections needed a little extra filing at the corners to square them up and make a tight fit. I carefully sanded the corner sections using a medium-grit sanding stick, **5-29**.

After assembling the walls, I installed a .040" sheet-styrene roof. I glued it in place with liquid plastic cement and, where the roof met the walls, reinforced the edges with .080"-square styrene strips. I then added an assortment of chimneys and vent pipes made from scrap styrene.

The windows and doors for the DPM walls are installed separately, and I waited to add mine until after I'd painted the factory.

STEP 4 Painting and making signs

I primed the factory and the warehouse with Rust-Oleum Light Gray Primer, an organic solvent-base spray primer. This was especially important for the wood Bar Mills structure because the primer seals the wood and prevents it from warping. I then airbrushed the factory brick red and painted the factory windows and the warehouse white. I brush-painted both roofs black and weathered them with powdered pastels.

Next, I installed the windows on the DPM kit and added dry transfer lettering for the company signs and slogans. I weathered the lettering using more powdered pastels, **5-30**.

To fade the color of brick walls and make the mortar lines stand out, I applied a wash of one part water-base white paint diluted in 10 parts of 70 percent rubbing alcohol. To apply the wash, I laid the model flat and then flowed the diluted paint on with a soft brush, **5-31**. Once the paint filled the mortar lines, I daubed the wall with a paper towel to remove most of the white from the surface.

STEP 5 Adding finishing details

To finish the buildings, I added window glazing, view blocks, and a few other details such as workers, crates, and pallets.

I used .010" styrene sheet for window glazing, employing my new-found favorite way to install it – Woodland Scenics Accent Glue. This water-base adhesive is made to hold figures and other details on layouts, but it also works well for window glazing. Simply brush it on the back of the window, let it dry until it becomes tacky, and then press the glazing sheet in place. Accent Glue won't damage clear plastic the way liquid styrene cement or CA will, and it bonds to almost any material, making it perfect for wood.

I added a view block of black construction paper, installing it behind the window glazing with more Accent Glue, **5-32**.

Finally, to bring the finished scene to life, I added some dock workers and a few pallets and crates, **5-33**. With that, the Quincy & Smith Pin Co. was ready to take its place on my layout.

PROJECT 4: Making a mix-and-match industry

Sometimes it's hard to get past the idea that the businesses on your layout look just like those on hundreds of other layouts. In addition to kitbashing, another way to avoid that "one with the rest of the model railroad universe" appearance is to mix and match kit parts to make your industries unique.

This mix-and-match approach isn't quite the same as the kitbashing technique used in projects 2 and 5. Instead of cutting up walls of an existing kit and reassembling them, I took parts, details, and complete structures from an assortment of manufacturers and

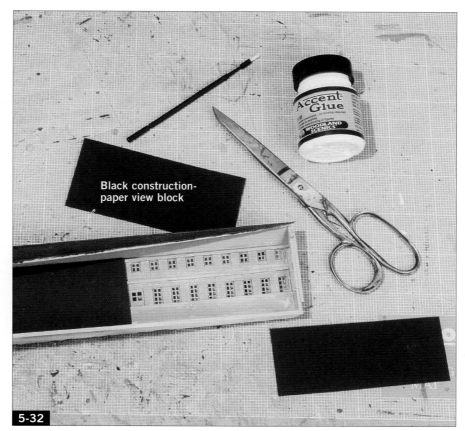

Black construction-paper view block

5-32

Woodland Scenics Accent Glue is ideal for cementing glazing to the backs of windows because it doesn't damage the clear plastic.

Black roof weathered with gray paint

LITY PINS SINCE 1864

Loading dock made from styrene scraps

5-33

Finishing details to the Quincy & Smith Pin Co. included a loading dock and dock workers.

5-34

Mixing pieces from various kits helps create unique-looking industries, such as this 1950s-era fuel dealer.

combined them to make a 1950s-era fuel dealer for my layout, **5-34**.

While you may not need a fuel dealership for your layout, you can apply the same mix-and-match techniques I used to create everything from small grain elevators to expansive industrial complexes.

STEP 1 Picking a prototype

Depending upon the era and region of the country you model, there are many ubiquitous lineside industries you could add to your railroad. Grain elevators in the Midwest are one such example. Perhaps an industry with more widespread appeal, however, is the fuel dealership.

Most early to mid-20th century fuel companies sold coal, heating oil, or both. (Modern versions sell heating oil and liquid petroleum gasses.) These products were delivered in bulk by rail and then sold to consumers for fuel to heat their homes and businesses. In addition to fuel, many dealerships also sold lumber, sand, concrete, other building supply products, and gasoline (making for an

Bar Mills trestle

Model Power barrels

American Model Builders feeder barn

Classic Metal Works vehicles

Walthers fence sections

Walthers oil tanks and pump house

Dyna Models conveyor

5-35

The trick to mixing and matching an industry is to choose components that look as if they belong together.

amazingly combustible combination of products).

The inspiration for my fuel dealership came from a lumberyard I worked at while I was in college. Although the lumberyard was new, it had been built on the site of a former lumber and fuel company. The yard's rail spur passed over the piers from the original coal dock, and though the bins had been filled in with

earth years before, there was no mistaking what had once been there.

When creating any mix-and-match industry, you'll want to choose components that appear to belong together, **5-35**. Photos or first-hand experience are a big help in this step. The materials list on the next page gives the part numbers of the main components that make up my fuel company.

5-36

I built a pit for the fuel tanks out of styrene scraps and then, with a utility knife, cut away a layer of Sculptamold and foam insulation scenery to fit the pit.

Storage shed

Walthers oil tanks

Pump house

5-37

After gluing the pit to scenery and the tanks to the pit, I added a pump house, which was made of walls from a Walthers kit and some corrugated styrene.

STEP 2 Modeling oil tanks and a storage shed

My fuel dealership handles two basic commodities – fuel oil and coal. The oil side of the business includes a set of tanks, a pump house, and a large storage shed for barrels and the equipment necessary to keep the delivery trucks running. The shed also holds the company's office.

I used an American Model Builders feeder barn kit for the shed. Assemble the kit following the directions but add a floor made with foam board to keep the thin wood walls from bowing. Barn red was a common color for wood structures in that era. I painted mine that color with white doors and then heavily weathered the structure. To identify the industry as a fuel dealer, I added a few Blair Line printed signs and some dry transfer lettering.

The rest of the oil plant is made from leftover pieces of a Walthers

Goldenflame Fuel Co. kit I'd used on a different part of the layout. The oil tanks (included in the kit) are modular, and you can make them different heights by varying the number of rings you use. I built two tanks with four rings each and one taller tank using five rings. Paint the tanks white with a little rust weathering.

Many oil tanks have a retention berm or pit. I built a pit from styrene scraps, modeling it after concrete berms I'd seen in my hometown.

To install the pit, trace its footprint on the layout's surface. Next, cut away a thin layer of the scenery, **5-36**. After test-fitting the pit, glue it to the scenery using latex caulk, then cement the tanks in place with CA.

Near the oil tanks is the pump house, the walls of which came from the Walthers kit, **5-37**. Unfortunately, the kit doesn't include a roof. You can make a new roof for the house from .030" cor-

rugated styrene sheet. I painted my pump house gray to represent bare metal, but you may want to paint it the same red as the shed, giving both a company look.

STEP 3 Building a coal dock

The coal dock is a Bar Mills wood trestle kit. Build the trestle following the instructions but leave the cross bracing off the open side, so the coal trucks can be loaded, **5-38**. I cemented a piece of Peco code 55 flextrack to the trestle and then soldered a Tomar Industries Hayes

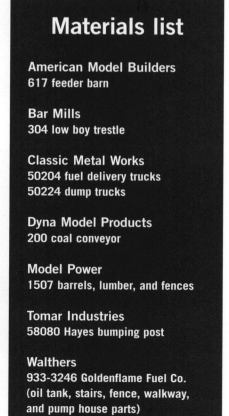

Materials list

American Model Builders
617 feeder barn

Bar Mills
304 low boy trestle

Classic Metal Works
50204 fuel delivery trucks
50224 dump trucks

Dyna Model Products
200 coal conveyor

Model Power
1507 barrels, lumber, and fences

Tomar Industries
58080 Hayes bumping post

Walthers
933-3246 Goldenflame Fuel Co.
(oil tank, stairs, fence, walkway, and pump house parts)

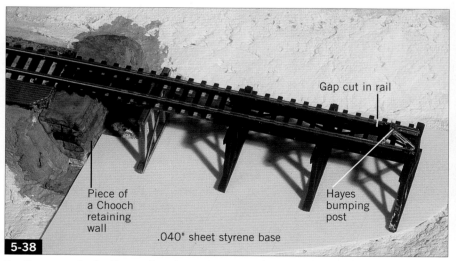

Gap cut in rail

Piece of a Chooch retaining wall

.040" sheet styrene base

Hayes bumping post

5-38

To allow space for loading coal trucks on the dock, build the trestle with only back bracing.

5-39

To fill a coal dock, first cut foam insulation blocks, shape them with sandpaper to form piles, and place them between the trestle bents.

5-40

Paint the foam blocks black, sprinkle them with coal, and then cement the blocks in place.

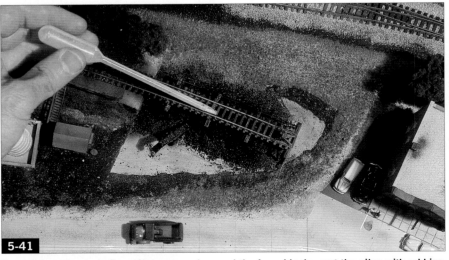

5-41

To complete the coal piles, sift loose coal around the foam blocks, wet the piles with rubbing alcohol, and cement the coal in place.

bumping post to the rails at the end of the track. If you use this bumper, be sure to cut a gap in one rail to prevent the metal bumping post from causing a short circuit (see chapter 3).

The trestle sits on a .040" sheet styrene base. After cutting the base to fit the coal unloading area, use a straight-edge and a hobby knife to score the styrene to look like individually poured concrete sections. Paint the styrene a concrete color.

For a retaining wall at the end of the fill leading up to the coal trestle, I used a piece cut from a Chooch stone wall. You could also make a retaining wall out of styrene or build it from pieces of stripwood.

After test fitting all the components, paint the parts and cement them to the layout.

At this point, it's a good idea to finish the surrounding scenery.

STEP 4 Filling the coal dock

Filling the coal dock is a bit trickier than it may seem at first. Though you could simply pile crushed coal to appropriate heights under the dock, you'd be using a lot of material. And piles of fine scenery materials don't often hold up well on a layout because the cement settles to the bottom, causing the top to eventually crumble apart. As a better alternative, fill the coal bins with small foam insulation blocks and then cover them with a thin, well-cemented layer of coal.

Cut and sand blocks of foam to form piles, fitting them between each of the trestle bents, **5-39**.

Next, paint the blocks black and sprinkle crushed coal onto the wet paint. (I used Woodland Scenics Mine Run Coal.) Cement the coal-covered blocks in position, **5-40**.

Finally, sift more coal over the top of the blocks with a spoon to fill the gaps between the bents and to blend the piles into the surrounding scenery. Carefully wet the coal piles with a few drops of rubbing alcohol and bond the loose coal in place with Scenic Cement from Woodland Scenics, **5-41**.

When the coal piles have dried, add some final details such as people, barrels, vehicles, and a conveyer or two. Your fuel dealer is now open for business.

5-42

When track runs close to a layout's edge, adding a fascia-hanging industry provides the space needed to add an extra set of structures.

PROJECT 5:
Expanding into the aisle

Where do you go when you need that extra bit of space on your layout for another track or an additional industry? Try expanding into the aisle.

On my layout, in addition to several larger businesses in the town of Prospect Hill, I had room for a single spur along the fascia but no space for an industry. I decided the spur would serve a brass stamping plant, receiving and shipping carloads of appropriate materials. The track, however, was a bit too close to the edge of the layout. And try as I might to make myself believe that there really was an industry next to the spur, I wasn't satisfied with the structure's transparent quality.

As a result, I added a fascia-hanging industry, **5-42**. This narrow set of structures simply bumps out from the fascia several inches into the aisle, adding the visual satisfaction of having actual structures along the spur while providing edge safety for the rolling stock parked there.

A fascia-hanging industry is easy to build, and with a bit of careful planning, you can add one to just about any model railroad.

STEP 1 Building a mock-up

When deciding to add an industry along the fascia, height and width are important considerations. On most model railroads, aisle space is already at a premium, so you don't want to encroach too much into that territory. A fascia-hanging complex that's too

5-43

By photocopying kit parts and taping them together, you can make mock-up structures.

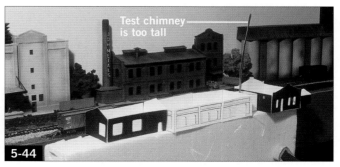

5-44

Clamping a piece of foam to the layout gives you a temporary fascia bump on which to discover any potential problems.

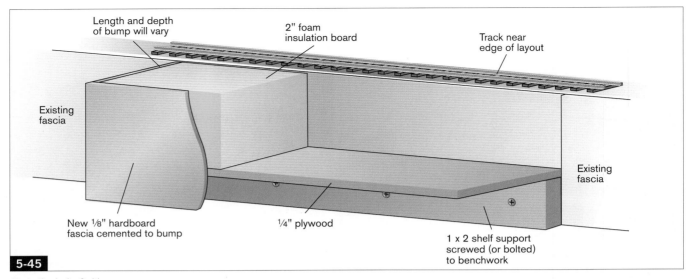

Length and depth
of bump will vary

2" foam
insulation board

Track near
edge of layout

Existing
fascia

Existing
fascia

New ⅛" hardboard
fascia cemented to bump

¼" plywood

1 x 2 shelf support
screwed (or bolted)
to benchwork

5-45

Illustration by Jay Smith

wide will stand a good chance of being damaged. And since it's in the foreground, you'll want the structures to be low enough so operators can easily reach over them.

To make sure the height and width will work before investing the time in building the structures, you can make a mock-up. I built my brass stamping plant mock-up by photocopying the kit pieces I planned on using. I then cut out the paper parts and taped them together, **5-43**. This is a great way to avoid making mistakes later when you start cutting kit components.

After completing your paper mock-up, move it to the layout for a test fitting, **5-44**. You can make a temporary base by clamping a piece of foam insulation to the layout edge. Though my buildings were low enough for operators to reach and see over, I quickly discovered that the chimney was going to need some adjustment.

STEP 2 Adding the bump

Once you're happy with how the mock-up structures fit into the layout, it's time to build the bump in the fascia. You can make it either a permanent installation or a removable feature. If you want to make it removable, I'd recommend using fasteners, such as carriage bolts and wing nuts, to hold it in place. Since the extension sticks out into the aisle, there's a good chance that once in a while the bump could be, well, bumped. By attaching it with carriage bolts and wing nuts, you can still remove it should the need arise.

For my fascia-hanging industry, I permanently attached the bump to the existing benchwork, **5-45**. It sits on a simple plywood shelf screwed to a 1 x 2 support block. The mounting block is bolted to the fascia. I then used foam insulation board to build the area up to the layout's track height.

You can make the bump match the

rest of your layout by simply covering it with the same fascia material. I covered mine with ⅛" hardboard, cementing it to the foam with latex construction adhesive.

STEP 3 Fabricating the factory

With the base in place, it's time to build the industry. My brass stamping plant is made from a collection of models, including a Faller no. 222180 freight house, a Heljan no. 641 freight station, and a Model Power no. 1566 Coverall Paints kit. I used the paper mock-up from step 1 as a guide for kitbashing the structures, **5-46**.

Because of the height and width issues involved with having this industry in the foreground, I made a lot of modifications to the kits, **5-47**. I made the boiler house from the Faller kit, building it without its baseplate and shortening the building's length by one third. I built the main factory section

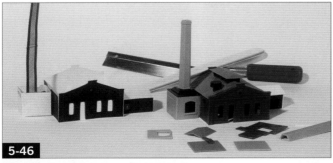

5-46

I modified the boiler house by eliminating the baseplate, shortened the building's length, and cut the chimney in half to make it easy to reach over.

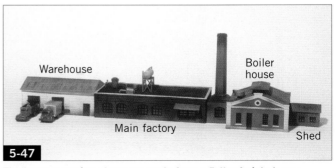

Warehouse

Boiler
house

Main factory

Shed

5-47

The brass stamping plant was made from a Faller freight house (boiler house), Heljan freight station (warehouse and shed), and a Model Power Coverall Paints factory (main factory).

from the Model Power kit but made it only one story tall. I used the spare second-floor wall sections to make the factory longer. The roof is made from .040" sheet styrene, and the rooftop tanks and piping came with the kit.

I used the Heljan kit for the warehouse, narrowing it a bit by building it without the surrounding loading docks and baseplate. I made new, narrower docks from styrene strips. The kit included some open overhead doors, so I added a styrene-sheet floor inside the model. The office from this kit became the boiler house shed, and both the warehouse and the shed got new styrene-sheet corrugated metal roofs.

STEP 4 Installing industries

Once your industry structures are complete, it's time to add them to the layout. I shaped the surrounding scenery with Sculptamold and then pressed the buildings into the wet material, **5-48**. This technique establishes a tight-fitting, level base for your buildings and eliminates the need to later hide gaps between the foundation and ground. At the same time, I also added a styrene sidewalk in front of the entry area, pressing it into the Sculptamold as well.

Once the Sculptamold dried, I carefully removed the buildings and painted the surrounding area and sidewalk. I then replaced the models and added the gravel driveway, track ballast, ground-foam turf, trees, and shrubs, **5-49**.

The final step is adding the finishing details to give your industry that lived-in look. I added an assortment of crates, boxes, and workers in the open warehouse doorways, **5-50**. I also included some trucks and cars in the parking lot to give the impression of activity. (We'll look more closely at detailing scenes in chapter 6.)

With the work complete, switching cars to the stamping plant is a lot more fun now that I can actually see it. And because of the added aisle-side real estate, there's no danger of the cars accidentally leaving the layout! If you're looking for this industry on the track plan on page 15, you'll find it has been surrounded by scenery and is labeled "Brass Stamping Plant."

5-48 Pressing the buildings into the wet Sculptamold scenery base provides a tight-fitting, level base.

5-49 After painting the scenery, glue landscaping details such as ballast, gravel, and weeds around the factory.

5-50 Give your industry a lived-in look by adding finishing details. I added trucks, workers, crates, rooftop fixtures, and an awning.

6-1

CHAPTER SIX

Detailing your model railroad, inside and out

Imagine how empty this scene would be without the vehicles, lumber, road signs, and figures. These types of details give your layout that lived-in look.

By the time you've laid and ballasted the track, formed hills and rivers, cemented grass and trees in place, and built an assortment of structures, your model railroad will start to look like a world in miniature. However, after a while, you'll probably notice that something about your layout doesn't seem quite right.

While the real estate prices may be attractive, you eventually discover that your businesses and homes are vacant. That lumberyard, which sees a lot of rail traffic, mysteriously keeps all its products hidden from view. The stores on Main Street look generic, leaving one to guess whether they sell hardware, haircuts, shoes, or anything at all. Everything is too quiet for comfort.

Details are the cure for the common-looking layout. People, vehicles, signs, and even recorded sounds give your layout a lived-in feeling, **6-1**. The best way to start a project like this one is by listening to and looking at the world around you or by finding some photos of the location and period that you're modeling. Then try to emulate what you see and hear.

PROJECT 1: Including ordinary details of everyday life

The women hanging wash on the back porch of a tenement check that the wind doesn't blow soot from the locomotive on their clean sheets. Kids playing baseball in the empty lot use an old pallet as a backstop. A police officer, making sure all is well in the neighborhood, drives his cruiser down a nearby street. And an engineer leans on the sill of his locomotive's open cab window, enjoying the warm autumn afternoon.

These details, **6-2**, are just a few of the things that are considered a part of everyday life. They seem common to us, yet that's exactly why they're important features to add to a model railroad. If you omit the ordinary, your scenes won't seem quite right to observers. However, include them on your layout, and you've succeeded in making your modeled world that much more realistic.

STEP 1 Populating a layout

Whether you purchase your model citizens in neatly painted sets or buy unpainted figures and color them yourself, figures are easy to add to your layout. To cement them in place, you can use cyanoacrylate adhesive, Walthers Goo, or Woodland Scenics Accent Glue.

Surprisingly, you don't really need a lot of figures on your model railroad to convey the idea that your layout is populated. If you can see a few people in a scene, your mind logically assumes there are others nearby. All it takes to make a coal dealership look like a busy industry are a truck driver, paperwork in hand, and a laborer leaning on his shovel, **6-3**.

Don't forget that vehicles need drivers. A road full of empty cars, just like an empty sidewalk, doesn't look right. Many model automobiles have some type of interior, making it easy to add drivers and passengers. For my Classic Metal Works vehicles, I disassembled each one, painted the interior, and added a seated figure or two, **6-4**. You may need to cut away part of the interior or figure to get them to fit.

6-2

By adding a few everyday details, the city of Waterbury, Conn., of the 1950s comes to life.

6-3

It only takes two figures to show activity at the coal dealership.

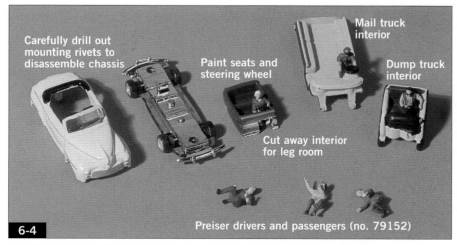
6-4

A road full of cars without drivers looks out of place. With a little modification, you can install figures in most model automobiles.

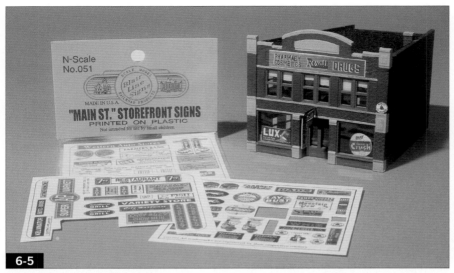

6-5

"Main St." Storefront Signs includes signs for a variety of businesses and products commonly advertised in the 1950s including Rexall Drugs, Lux Detergent, and Orange Crush.

6-6

This New Haven billboard, made from a Bar Mills kit, took less than an hour to assemble and paint.

6-7

Warning, caution, and regulatory signs add an authentic look to roadways.

STEP 2 Marketing businesses

We're a culture that thrives on advertising, and your layout will look naked without it. Though you can make your own signs from magazine, newspaper, or even phone book ads, a number of paper, styrene, dry transfer, and decal products are available to paste advertising to just about anything on your layout.

I used several different sets of signs from Blair Line for the storefronts on my railroad, 6-5. The full-color signs are printed on thin sheets of styrene and are available for a number of different eras. They're easy to cut out with a hobby knife or scissors, and you can glue the signs to your buildings using CA or white glue. Don't use liquid plastic cement because it may dissolve the thin styrene and damage the printing.

Another common form of business marketing is the billboard. To earn a bit of extra money, the owners of the produce warehouse on my layout rented out some of their rooftop space to the New Haven for advertising, 6-6. I added this railroad billboard to the structure using a Bar Mills kit. The kit is made from laser-cut wood and comes with neatly printed logos and graphics. It was so easy to build, I assembled and painted it at the office during lunch one day.

STEP 3 Making street improvements

In addition to advertising, we require an amazing number of signs to tell us what to do when we drive. A trip down almost any American highway could lead a foreign visitor to believe we are incapable of operating motor vehicles without a sign to tell us where we are, which way to go, which way the road turns, and what points of interest we are about to miss.

There are a host of road signs offered to model railroaders, and they're available for different eras as well. On my layout, I used several Blair Line road sign kits. Like the storefront signs, the road signs are printed on

6-8

To add guard rails, paint black rings on a .020" styrene rod, cut the rod with a side cutter, drill mounting holes with a pin vise at ⅜" intervals, and cement them with white glue.

thin styrene sheets. Each set comes with wood posts, but there are far more signs than posts in the kit. I made extra posts from .020" square styrene strips. Before assembling the signs, I painted the posts and the back of the signs gray to give them a more realistic appearance. Then I placed the finished signs, along with the cars and drivers from step 1, on the layout, **6-7**.

Guardrails are another important roadside detail. I really like the old black-and-white post-type guardrails used between the 1930s and '50s, so I made some for my layout. To make them in N scale, start by painting black rings, spaced ⅜" apart, around a .010" styrene rod. Next, cut the individual posts off the rod with a side cutter and glue them along your roadway at ⅜" intervals, **6-8**. Leave the white styrene tops exposed to simulate the guard posts' reflective white paint.

STEP 4 Detailing daily life

Items like tree swings and laundry hanging on wash lines are some of the details associated with everyday life. I made these two details for my layout, starting with two unlikely sources: plastic fishing poles and wood signposts, **6-9**.

I had purchased Preiser's Women Hanging Wash (no. 79050) but was dis-

Where to find details

No matter what scale you've chosen, there's a vast assortment of details available for your model railroad. Looking for people? Try figures from Preiser, Woodland Scenics, or Noch. Need some 1950s vintage cars? Classic Metal Works is a good place to start for HO or N scale vehicles. How about garbage cans or baggage carts – Detail Associates and Period Miniatures have some nice models to choose from.

You'll find there are many railroad right-of-way details available as well. Line poles, switch stands, trackside junk, speeder sheds, and signals are all easy to obtain, both as kits or as ready-to-use items.

Where do you find all this stuff? Pick up a copy of any Wm. K. Walthers catalog at your local hobby shop or visit www.walthers.com and you'll find enough listings for figures, vehicles, detail items, and signs to keep you busy for hours.

New wash line

Swing

Fishing poles

Sign posts

6-9

With a little improvisation, some CA, and extra parts, you can add interesting everyday details to a layout, such as wash lines and tree swings.

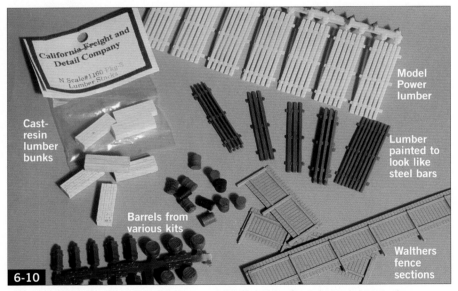

California Freight and Detail Company

N Scale #1160 Pkg-3 Lumber Stocks

Model Power lumber

Cast-resin lumber bunks

Lumber painted to look like steel bars

Barrels from various kits

Walthers fence sections

6-10

Barrels, crates, oil drums, steel beams, and fences are details that can enhance almost any industry.

your layout, you could use fine piano wire or brass rod.

STEP 5 Adding products for industry

Because of the size and number of products they handle, industries such as lumberyards and foundries usually leave a lot of materials laying around outdoors. As a result, these businesses tend to look vacant if their surroundings are too clean.

To add bunks of wood to my lumberyard, **6-1**, I used resin castings made by California Freight and Detail Co. (no. 1160). The castings have nice detail and come painted in a bare-wood tone. I'd originally planned to use a Model Power milled lumber kit (no. 1507) but found that the boards were too large for those stocked by a typical N scale lumberyard. (They'd look good on an HO layout though.) However, by painting the stacks of thinner boards several shades of gray and rust, I made a nice assortment of metal parts for my foundry, **6-10**.

You may also be surprised to find that you already have good industrial detail parts. Structure kits often come with a wealth of useful items, such as the board fence sections from the Walthers Goldenflame Fuel Co. kit (no. 3246), **6-10**. Other kits can include barrels, oil drums, and boxes.

PROJECT 2: Producing quick mainline details

If you look at some photos, or glance around a stretch of your favorite main line, you'll see that real railroads have a lot more to them than just track and trains. In fact, you'll soon discover that there is a host of details that you can easily add to your layout to make it more prototypical, **6-11**.

It didn't take much to dress up my layout's main line – I've included five easy steps in this project to get you started. For a more in-depth study of trackside details, pick up a copy of *Trackwork and Lineside Detail for Your Model Railroad* from Kalmbach Books.

appointed in the thick wash line. At the same time, I'd also bought some Preiser N scale fishermen (no. 79077) that come with lengths of thin, black plastic rod for making fishing poles. By combining a plastic fishing pole with some wood posts from a Blair Line road sign kit, you can make a finer-scale wash line.

Start by drilling no. 80 holes near the post tops and slide the plastic rod through the holes and cement it in

place with CA to form the rope line. Next, cut the plastic clothes from the Preiser wash line and cement them in place on the new one. The finished model has the correct lightness to it, making it more realistic.

You can also make a tree swing using the same materials. Use a small piece of wood post for the seat and two lengths of pole material for the swing's ropes. If you don't need fisherman for

6-11

Crossbucks and line poles are simple things you can add along a main line to make it more prototypical.

STEP 1 Placing line poles

Line poles, often called telephone or telegraph poles, were once the information arteries of railroading, carrying signal and track condition data as well as allowing train-order operators and other railroad workers to communicate. The role of the line pole has been greatly diminished, or phased out altogether, and many railroads have simply left them where they stand – in use or not. As a result, line poles have been

(and continue to be) a common main-line feature for more than 125 years.

There aren't many choices for ready-to-use N scale line poles (I like Rix Products poles for HO scale applications), but with some modifications, the Atlas no. 2801 telephone pole works well, **6-12**. I painted the poles Polly Scale New Gravel Gray and weathered them with a wash of Engine Black. I then painted the insulators either white or green to represent glass.

Poles follow the right-of-way on either the left side or right side (sometimes both) and often lean, especially these days. Although real line poles are spaced somewhere between 132 and 203 feet apart (depending upon the railroad), model poles look better if set closer together. A good rule of thumb is to plant N scale poles at 6" intervals (12" for HO scale), roughly 80 to 90 scale feet apart, **6-13**.

6-12

To prepare poles for planting, first clip off their bases, remove or shorten some crossarms, and then paint the poles.

6-13

For the best placement, space N scale poles 6" apart, about 80-90 scale feet, along the tracks.

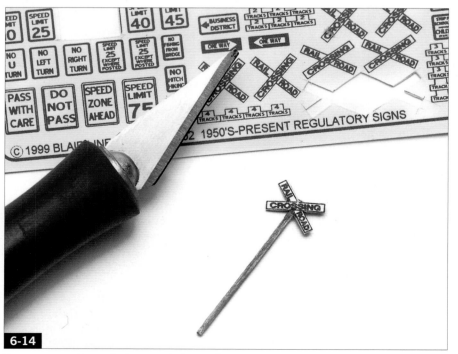

6-14

For easy assembly, stain the posts before gluing on the styrene signs.

STEP 2 Installing grade crossings

Anywhere a railroad crosses a street, road, or private drive at grade, it needs to be marked to alert motorists of potential train traffic. The simplest solution is to install a warning sign called a crossbuck, a post with crossed white signs that read "railroad crossing."

To add crossbucks to my layout, I used Blair Line's sign kit no. 2, which includes scale-sized wood posts and a sheet of printed styrene signs, **6-14**. After staining the wood posts with a driftwood-colored paint thinned with rubbing alcohol, I cut out the styrene signs and glued them in place with CA.

Minor street intersections may have a crossbuck with one or more flashing or waving red lights, and major intersections receive additional protection with gates. I installed NJ International crossing gates (no. 2163) on two such streets. The signals come with movable gates and are wired with LEDs so they could be made operational. In my case, however, I chose to simply install them as is, gluing a straight pin into the base, **6-15**. The pins hold the crossing gates securely to the scenery yet make them removable during track cleaning.

STEP 3 Adding instrument cases

From the time when railroads added signaling in the late 1800s, instrument cases have been a regular trackside feature. The most common type used in the past 75 years is a sheet-metal structure mounted on a concrete base. Instrument cases (also called relay houses or bungalows) are typically located near the signals and grade crossings they serve. A round or square battery well (the covered concrete box that holds the batteries that power the equipment) stands next to each case or group of cases.

I picked up two packages of N scale lineside details from Railway Express Miniatures (nos. 2141 and 2151) that included metal castings for four different sized instrument cases. After filing away the flash and gluing the larger cases together with CA, I painted their foundations Polly Scale Concrete and the metal walls and roofs Polly Scale Aluminum. I weathered the models with a thin wash of black paint. I used a smaller instrument case for a grade crossing, **6-16**, and a larger case in a typical signal installation, **6-17**.

STEP 4 Installing switch stands

Switch stands are common trackside elements. Railroads use them to set the route through a manually controlled turnout and give train crews a visual indication of the position of the switch points. Railway Express Miniatures set no. 2141 includes three nonoperating switch stand castings that I installed on turnouts at industry spurs.

The switch stands can be mounted directly to the turnout's head blocks (the two long ties on either side of the switch rod) or on tie extensions added by the modeler. I glued the castings to strips of styrene matching the size of the ties of my Peco track, **6-18**. I painted the switch stand and tie assemblies Polly Scale Engine Black with Caboose Red targets, **6-19**. Once the paint had dried, I cemented the stands in place with CA, **6-20**.

The castings come with a typical diamond target, but switch stand targets can be as individual as the railroad itself, so consulting photos of your favorite prototype is a good idea. Most switch stand targets can be modeled with small pieces of styrene, though if you're not fussy, you can leave the diamond targets as they come.

STEP 5 Finishing with phone boxes and piles of stuff

In addition to the instrument cases and switch stands, the two packages of Railway Express Miniatures detail parts also contain other commonly found trackside items including a phone box, a cluster of track part buckets (used to hold bolts, tie plates, and spikes), and piles of ties and culverts.

In the days before radios, phone boxes were located at key points along a railroad's right-of-way – typically at track intersection points such as sidings, passing tracks, and crossings. Railroad phones were usually housed in small, post-mounted instrument cases or in wood or metal booths. The phone box in the detail parts set is the post-mounted variety, and I placed it at one end of a passing siding, **6-21**.

6-15

A nonoperational crossing gate can be held to scenery by using a mounting pin glued in the base with CA.

6-16

A battery well and instrument case will be located near almost every grade crossing signal and gate.

6-17

Railroad signals will also have instrument cases nearby. I've placed this large relay case next to the location for a future block signal.

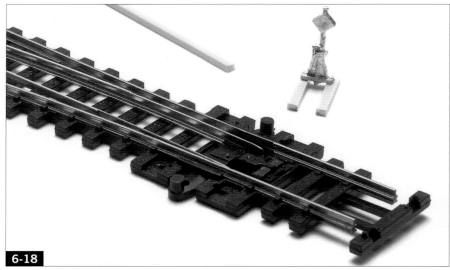

6-18

On this Peco turnout, I made styrene tie extensions that matched the size of the turnout's ties for mounting the switch stand.

6-19

I painted the stand and ties black and the target Caboose Red.

6-20

When cementing switch stands in place, be sure to set them far enough back to clear trains.

6-21

This metal post-mounted phone box features a simulated concrete base. Many were simple wood boxes bolted directly to a line pole.

6-22

Culverts, ties, and part buckets are common trackside features, particularly near where a track gang has been working.

Other trackside details include railroad construction materials such as piles of ties and spike buckets. These items were typically gathered outside a section gang's headquarters as a stockpile. After painting the Railway Express Miniatures castings, I placed the ties, culverts, and track part buckets in an empty space behind a station, **6-22**.

You could also add spare switch stands, crossbucks, crossing gate arms, instrument cases, and stacks of rusty rail cut into 39-scale-foot lengths – all things that may be needed by railroad maintenance workers.

6-23

Building a detailed train station scene, such as the Prospect Hill depot, can be completed in a week of evening projects.

PROJECT 3: Putting together a station scene

One thing that most people can relate to on a model railroad is a depot scene. Like a grade crossing, a train station is one of those few places where the public interacts directly with railroads.

There once was a time in the lives of many communities when the town train station was the main connection with the outside world – whether you needed to ship a parcel, pick up a relative, or take a trip to the city, all of these things were done at the local depot. Though times have changed quite a bit since then, in metropolitan areas where mass transit is used, you

Trackside detail modeling tips

- Model line poles look best spaced 80 to 90 scale feet apart, which translates to approximately 6" for N scale and 12" for HO.

- Adding mounting pins to details such as crossing gates gives them a better chance of surviving bumps from full-size operators and makes details close to the right-of-way removable when cleaning track.

- Grade crossings and block signals should have an instrument case and a battery well nearby.

- Derelict items such as line poles and instrument cases are often left in place for years before a railroad removes them.

- Maintenance details such as part buckets, culverts, ties, and spare rails can be found near the tracks anywhere a track gang may be stationed.

Cork used to support platform and depot

6-24

After gluing the cork roadbed in place, fill in the surrounding areas with spackling compound to level the surrounding ground.

6-25

Before assembling the resin depot, clear away any flash remaining from the molding process, such as in the corners of window and door openings.

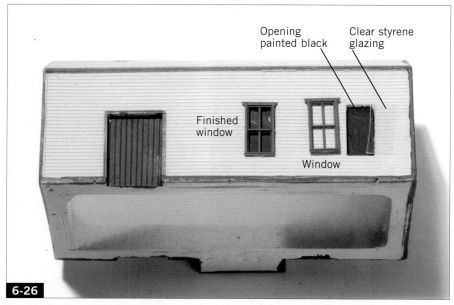

Opening painted black

Clear styrene glazing

Finished window

Window

6-26

To add windows to the depot, first paint the openings black, cement glazing to back of each window, and glue the windows over the openings.

can still see a lot of activity around a depot.

Sometimes detailing a scene requires more than just a few figures and cars. As an example, the depot scene at my town of Prospect Hill was pretty much built from the ground up as a single week-long project. **6-23**.

STEP 1 Leveling the ground

Before getting started, you'll need to know how much space your depot will take up, including room for platforms and parking. After figuring out the area I'd need for the passenger platform, I shopped around for depot kits that would fit the remaining space. I chose the Country Depot kit from Depots By John (available in both N and HO scales) because it had some of the architectural features I wanted.

Platform widths vary quite a bit, depending upon the railroad and the location, but I've found that in N scale, I can get a good-size station platform using one strip of ⅛" N scale cork roadbed for a base. (Use two strips for an HO scale platform). Once you've determined where the platform and station will be located, cement the strip of roadbed for the platform in place with carpenter's glue. Then use additional strips of cork to build a smooth, level foundation for the station. Pin the cork in place until the glue dries and then fill in the surrounding area to bring the scenery up to the correct level, **6-24**. I use Dap One-Time spackling because it's easy to work with and dries quickly.

Once the spackling has dried, paint this new ground with the same paint you used for the rest of the scenery.

STEP 2 Building a simple resin kit

The Depots-by-John kit comes as a single resin casting with separate plastic windows, doors, roofing materials, and cast-metal details. The main structure is a hollow block with the trim, siding, and freight doors cast in place. Though it has indentations for window openings, it would be difficult to build the model with a detailed interior. Instead, interior depth is created by illusion (explained in step 3).

Start by cleaning the resin casting. There will be some flash left behind from the molding process as well as some excess resin in the corners of the window and door openings. It can be removed quickly and easily using a sharp hobby knife and a small file, **6-25**. Once you've cleaned up the resin block, wash it in mild soapy water and rinse it thoroughly to remove any grease and remaining mold release agents before painting it.

The roof for the kit is made from sheet styrene and covered with thin sheet-styrene shingles. Cut the styrene roof first, and then use it as a pattern for cutting the shingles. Cement the shingles to the styrene with CA but don't attach the roof to the station just yet. Paint the depot, roof, and windows separately before assembly. I painted my depot Polly Scale SCL Hopper Car Beige and used Roof Brown for the windows, doors, and trim. The shingles are painted UP Dark Gray.

STEP 3 Finishing the depot

With the paint dry, you can assemble the depot. Begin by painting the window openings black, **6-26**. Next, assemble the windows by carefully cementing a piece of clear styrene sheet to the back of each casting with an adhesive such as Woodland Scenics Accent Cement, a water soluble contact cement. (Avoid using an adhesive that will fog the clear styrene.) Once the window and its clear glazing are cemented in front of the black opening, the depot will appear hollow.

This is also a good time to add some station signs, **6-27**, which you can make on your home computer. I cemented the signs to the building with Accent Cement. Finally, cement the roof, cast-metal brackets, and chimney in place. CA works well for these parts.

STEP 4 Building the platform

Now it's time to cover the cork platform and station foundation. I used Kibri no. 7960 cobblestone sheet for this part of the project. I started by making a paper pattern of the platform area (I also included the depot base). Then I set a sheet of paper over the cork platform and rubbed the edges with a pencil to mark the outline on the paper. Next, I taped the pattern to

6-27
Before cementing the roof in place, add paper station signs to the depot walls.

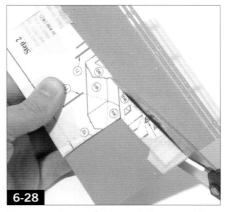
6-28
A paper pattern (mine's made from an old kit instruction sheet) aids in cutting the Kibri cobblestone sheet that makes up the platform surface.

6-29
Add the platform railings and retaining wall before painting the platform.

the plastic cobblestone material and cut out the platform with a scissors, **6-28**. You may need to sand or file the cobblestones a little to get a good fit.

Along the track side of the platform is a wood retaining wall made from railroad ties. You can use a number of different materials to make this wall, including wood ties. I used a strip of styrene, scoring it every ⅝" to simulate the ties. I cemented it to the front of the cobblestone sheet with liquid plastic cement.

Some railroads use sections of railing or ornate fencing along the backs of their platforms, **6-29**. On my platform, I cemented sections of railing along the back edges, making the railing from some plastic pieces left over from an old Con-Cor gravel crusher kit. A number of manufacturers make scale railing and fence sections including Gold Medal Models and Plastruct, and these make good substitutes.

Cement the finished platforms to the cork with an acrylic latex caulk and then paint them. I painted the railings and the ties first, and then I painted the cobblestones Polly Scale Mineral Red. Once the paint dries, finish the surrounding scenery and parking lot.

STEP 5 Detailing the depot

Detailing the station is the best part of the project. There are a lot of details you can add to a station scene, depending upon the period you're modeling. For those working in N scale, Model Power set no. 1339 (also available in HO scale) has a nice assortment of benches, trash bins, mailboxes, fire hydrants, and a phone booth, **6-30**. All of these items can be found around a depot, and with a little weathering, they are great for adding life to an urban scene. I've used one or more of these sets for each station on my layout.

Another key railroad station item found in most eras is the green-and-red baggage cart. These carts, made of wood and steel, were close to the floor height of a typical baggage car, making it easy to load or unload the car quickly during short stops. When not in use, baggage carts usually sat alongside the station under the eaves to keep them protected from the weather. I used carts made by Period Miniatures (no. 2139). These brass and white metal-casting models are easy to assemble and paint.

Of course, you'll want to have passengers and a few automobiles around your station as well, **6-31**. Items like luggage, milk cans, and parcels waiting to be shipped out or picked up are also common features.

It doesn't take a lot of work to make a good-looking station scene for your layout, and your visitors (as well as your model passengers) will appreciate it.

PROJECT 4: Adding easy interior details

Structure windows can be frustrating for a modeler. Why are the panes such a pain, you may ask? Empty windows, especially the big ones found on storefronts, can break the illusion of a modeled world almost as fast as shiny plastic freight cars and locomotives.

In the real world, windows allow light into buildings, but they also allow passersby a glimpse inside. If you take a quick look around at houses, shops, factories, and offices, you'll find that many windows have curtains, shades, or blinds to keep people from looking in. Though you can't see much beyond these view blocks, the curtains and blinds themselves are usually visible from the outside.

Where windows are left open, you will be able to see some interior detail. This is especially true with storefronts, where a front window is used as display and advertising space. And unless the windows are boarded up, empty buildings show some type of interior detail, even if it's bare walls, rubbish, and cardboard boxes.

With a little styrene, some paint, and a few signs and figures, making simple interior details for your model railroad structures is easy, **6-32**. And they can be added to new kits and assembled buildings alike.

6-30

Along with a baggage cart from Period Miniatures, I used Model Power station details to add life to a train depot scene.

6-31

Passengers and automobiles complete the station detailing and give it a feeling of activity.

STEP 1 Building basic walls

It adds to the realism of the model structure if viewers can't see all the way through the building. As explained in chapter 5, one method is to place a view block inside the finished model. I placed black construction paper at an angle so viewers can't look in the upper windows, **6-33**. If you're working with a bigger structure, you might use card-stock or black styrene.

Though it's great for buildings with small windows, the black view-block trick doesn't work well for large windows, especially in storefronts. In this case, you're better off making simple walls from styrene. I use .030" sheet styrene to divide the storefront from the back of the building and partition separate building entrances, such as stairwells. I also add a styrene ceiling to the first floor to prevent a view of the store from the second-floor windows.

I typically add the walls and ceiling while the building is under construction and then paint them solid colors.

6-32

Mel's Cafe includes styrene walls and floors, furniture, and figures to give the interior a realistic look.

If you're adding walls to an existing building, you could make them as a freestanding unit that slips inside the building's shell, **6-33**.

STEP 2 Constructing simple interiors

Adding three-dimensional interiors to easily viewed structures provides a lot of interest to your model railroad. This is a fun project, and you don't have to go to dollhouse-level detailing to get good results. I built these three interiors for structures on my layout, using an assortment of styrene shapes to give the impression of chairs, sofas, and desks. I then painted them appropriate colors and added a few figures to bring the scenes to life. When seen from the edge of the layout, these details go a long way in convincing people that all the buildings have interiors.

I used styrene to make the interior for my N Scale Architect New Haven interlocking tower, **6-34**. I used grooved sheet styrene to represent the wood floor. I added a Period Minia-

tures coal stove casting and then made a desk from several pieces of strip styrene. The interlocking mechanism is made from sections of plastic Con-Cor fencing. Up close, the finished model looks only a little like a real interlocking plant, but when viewed from outside the building, just the levers are clearly visible, which provides the illusion that everything is correct.

For the drugstore (DPM no. 503), I filled the shop windows with signs and built a small apartment scene for the second floor, **6-35**. I used styrene shapes here to make a couch, chair, television, and table. After painting these details, I added some figures.

Mel's Cafe is another DPM kit (no. 512), **6-36**. I started the interior by walling off the stairwell and adding a back wall to the diner area. Next, I made a floor for the diner and modeled two booths, one for each window, from strip styrene. I painted most of the interior a wood color and then added a few figures and an Open sign for the window.

.030" styrene walls

Black-paper view block

Stairwell

6-33

The freestanding interior unit of this music store features walls, a view block, and a stairwell.

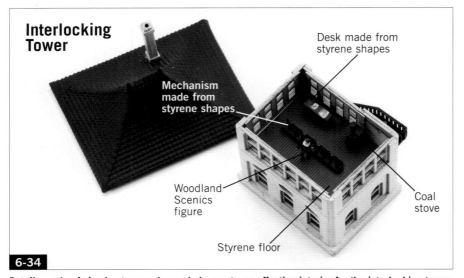

Interlocking Tower

Mechanism made from styrene shapes

Desk made from styrene shapes

Woodland Scenics figure

Coal stove

Styrene floor

6-34

Details made of simple styrene shapes help create an effective interior for the interlocking tower.

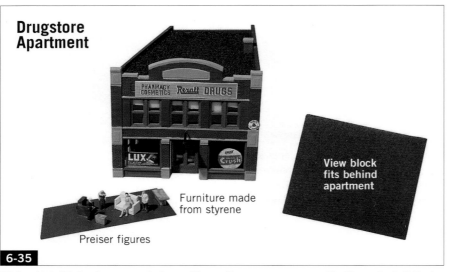

Drugstore Apartment

PHARMACY COSMETICS *Rexall* DRUGS

LUX

Crush

Furniture made from styrene

View block fits behind apartment

Preiser figures

6-35

While signs fill the drugstore windows, this small apartment scene adds life to the building's second floor.

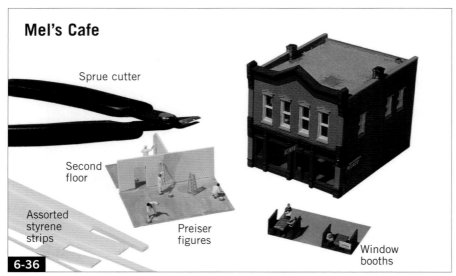

Mel's Cafe

Sprue cutter

Second floor

Assorted styrene strips

Preiser figures

Window booths

6-36

This cafe is close to the front edge of the layout, so it has detailed scenes on both floors.

This building has a detailed upstairs and features a Preiser no. 79176 painting crew. The floor and walls are made from .030" styrene. I left the walls white but added a few tan swatches, so it looks like the crew has just gotten started.

PROJECT 5: Adding sound to the layout

Of the five senses, after sight, sound plays the next biggest role in model railroading. Adding sound to a layout provides an extra layer of reality – when the scaled-down objects you're looking at make the noises you expect them to make, the modeled world becomes more realistic, **6-37**. Though you may think adding sound to your model railroad would be difficult, guess again. There are four different options for adding sound to your layout. All the projects described here involve installing small, self-powered media satellite speakers under the benchwork. And when you use high-quality sound recordings, the sound seems to come from everywhere.

Perhaps the most important part of adding effective sound to a model railroad is remembering to keep the volume in scale with the models. Though each of these projects involves amplified speakers, the best results come from running them at scale volume – which means low. Real locomotives or clock tower chimes are very loud when you stand right next to them, but that isn't how you relate to them on a layout. When you view your models up close at eye-level, you're still at least several hundred scale feet away, so the volume needs to be scaled down accordingly.

OPTION 1 Using self-contained sound systems

One way to quickly add sound to your model railroad is to use off-the-shelf, self-contained components. Model Rectifier Corp. (MRC), Noch, and a few other manufacturers make ready-to-use layout sound modules. The MRC Sound Station system comes with two powered speakers and a hand-held control unit, **6-38**. This particular system includes sounds of city

City traffic
Industrial activity
Flowing water
Idling locomotive
Birds

6-37

When the objects on a layout make the sounds you would expect them to, it adds another layer of reality.

6-38

One sound option is the ready-to-use MRC Sound Station, which comes with two powered speakers and a hand-held control unit. *Jim Forbes*

6-39

Playing sound effects CDs through a disk player and satellite speakers installed under a layout is another easy way to add sound. *Jim Forbes*

and country scenes, but MRC offers a railroad version as well.

The unit features two types of digital-sound files – continuous and short-duration. Continuous files repeat over and over when activated and include sounds such as stream noises, passing traffic, and gently falling rain. The MRC system also features an assortment of button-activated, short-duration sounds that play set patterns. This system includes sounds such as a barking dog, a car horn, a siren, and various farm animals.

The MRC system is an easy way to add sound to a model railroad, but it wasn't exactly what I was looking for.

OPTION 2 Playing sound-effects CDs

By installing an inexpensive compact disk player and a set of media satellite speakers under the layout or in the scenery, you can add continuous background sound almost as quickly as using a self-contained system.

After doing a little research, I came across a company called Fantasonics Engineering. The firm has provided sound for theme park attractions and museum displays for years and is now applying those techniques to its Scale Magic line for model railroad sound products. These are richly layered sound-effects tracks designed to represent sounds from different locations and industries and are era specific. After sampling the firm's CD sounds

on its Web site, www.fantasonics.com, I ordered the *Big City* and *Roundhouse/Switchyard* disks for the World War II era, the period closest to what I model.

According to Jim Wells from Fantasonics, the sound-effects tracks are created from a combination of actual recordings and studio-engineered sounds. On the city disk, along with the constant hum of traffic, a few of the random, distinct sounds you can pick out include crows, a Salvation Army band, a clock tower and carillon, pieces of conversations from passers-by, gusts of wind, and train crossing bells.

Adding these sounds to a layout is easy – you can use an inexpensive CD player and speakers, **6-39**. Fantasonics includes a detailed how-to booklet with your first purchase that explains speaker positioning and how to get the most out of adding scale sound effects to a layout.

The CDs include multiple tracks, each with a different mix of effects and background noises. You can set most CD players to play continuously, repeat one track, or randomly choose between all the tracks on a disk. Considering that each track is approximately six to seven minutes long, these disks offer a great variety of background sounds.

OPTION 3 Integrating interactive sound modules

Although CD sound effects are easy to use, they have at least one drawback. Every time you turn on your layout,

you need to reprogram the play selections. Also, the CD option doesn't allow for any real interactive features – once it's playing, it stays that way.

Because of these issues, I chose to use interactive sound modules on my layout. Pricom Design makes a solid-state audio playback system called the Dream Player, **6-40**. This player is designed for use with model railroads and provides high-quality stereo sound. You can use the Dream Player in a variety of ways to add as much or as little interactive sound to your layout as you wish. And unlike a CD player, when you turn on the Dream Player, it knows exactly what it should be doing.

The system plays .wav sound files stored on SD flash memory cards. Using

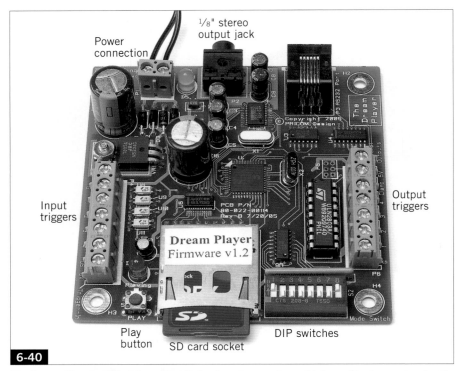

6-41

To load sound files onto the flash memory cards used by the Dream Player, you need a reader and a PC. *Jim Forbes*

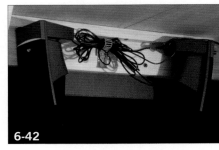

6-42

Dream Players require an amplified speaker system installed under the layout.

The Dream Player solid-state audio playback system produces high-quality stereo sound and allows for interactive operation. *Jim Forbes*

a simple card reader and a PC, you can load your own .wav files on the card (up to four tracks), **6-41**. Pricom offers an assortment of sound files on its Web site, www.pricom.com, as free downloads. (I tried these and enjoyed the ocean sound so much, I left it play on the computer in my office for a week!)

Dream Players require an amplified speaker system, and any powered satel-lite speaker set will work. I purchased two 14-watt sets with subwoofers for my players and got excellent results, **6-42**.

I used two Dream Players and speaker sets on my layout, one under the city of Waterbury and another under the rural river scene on the other end of the railroad. For the river scene, I ordered a 512MG SD card from Fantasonics loaded with its *Streams & Creeks* sounds.

I set this player to start playing when I turn on power to the layout, and it loops the 40-minute river track continuously.

For the Waterbury player, I loaded three .wav files on the card. The first two are from tracks on the Scale Magic *Big City* CD. The third comes from the *Roundhouse/Switchyard* disk, which I used to represent the industrial sounds for the brass manu-facturing plants in Waterbury. After converting these files to the .wav format, I placed them on the card as tracks 1, 2, and 3. (I left the fourth track open for future use.)

The Dream Player can have up to four external triggers (one for each track). These triggers can be push but-tons, motion sensors, photo cells, occu-pancy detectors, or DCC decoders. I used three momentary contact switches (Radio Shack no. 275-646) for this player, mounting them at various places on the fascia around the Waterbury peninsula, **6-43**.

When an operator pushes one of the two buttons on the city side of the peninsula, city noises play. If the opera-tor moves to switch the industrial side of town and pushes that button, the Dream Player fades out the city track

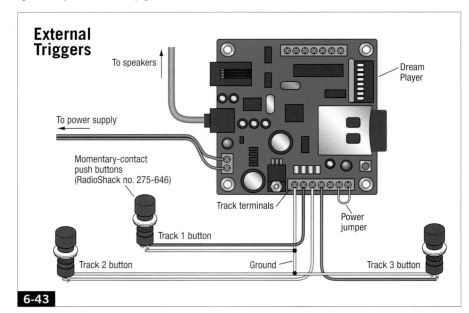

6-43

Illustration by Kellie Jaeger

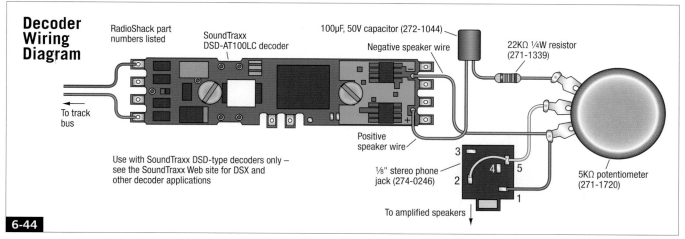

Decoder Wiring Diagram

RadioShack part numbers listed

SoundTraxx DSD-AT100LC decoder

100µF, 50V capacitor (272-1044)

22KΩ ¼W resistor (271-1339)

Negative speaker wire

To track bus

Positive speaker wire

Use with SoundTraxx DSD-type decoders only – see the SoundTraxx Web site for DSX and other decoder applications

⅛" stereo phone jack (274-0246)

To amplified speakers

5KΩ potentiometer (271-1720)

6-44

Illustration by Kellie Jaeger

and then starts the industry track. Fantasonics engineered the industry track to also include city noises in the background, so operators on either side get some of the proper sounds.

The Dream Players work wonderfully, and the sounds carry around the room enough so they blend well. When you're standing by the river scene, every so often you can hear the chimes of a distant clock tower from the city's player, which is a great effect!

OPTION 4 Using under-layout sound decoders

With the background sound effects in place, it was painfully obvious that the trains themselves were silent, so I started looking for locomotive sound options. Although it's possible to install sound in some N scale locomotives, it isn't nearly as easy or commonplace as it is in HO scale. And when you do fit a DCC sound decoder and speaker

into an N scale model, the sound quality is often disappointing.

My solution was to install a sound decoder and much bigger speakers under the layout for one locomotive. Since my Waterbury Yard switch engine (an Alco RS-1) always stays in the same area on the layout, I figured it would be a good candidate for this project.

I purchased a Soundtraxx DSD decoder with Alco sounds and downloaded the firm's instruction sheet for under-layout installations from its Web site, www.soundtraxx.com. The sheet includes a simple wiring diagram with RadioShack part numbers for the needed components.

I wired the components to the decoder, placed it all in a plastic 2" x 4" project box, **6-44**, and drilled a few holes in the box so the decoder could breathe.

Before mounting the box under the layout, I clipped the decoder's power leads to my programming track and

set the decoder's address to match my Waterbury switch engine, **6-45**. This way the locomotive's decoder and the under-layout sound decoder both respond to the same commands. I then wired the decoder to the yard track bus and mounted the project box under the layout, **6-46**.

For speakers, I mounted another satellite speaker set under the Waterbury Yard. I faced the speakers into the aisle, pointing toward the area where the yard engineer usually stands. I then fired up the switcher and adjusted the speaker volume until the locomotive sounded like it should for its size.

Admittedly, a single under-layout sound decoder is no substitute for a fleet of sound-equipped locomotives. However, even when my Alco yard switcher is parked and idling, its voice contributes significantly to the rest of the sounds around the layout, making my model railroad more enjoyable.

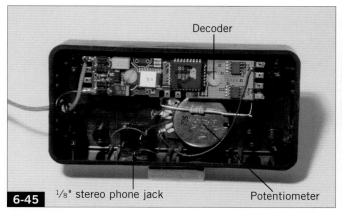

Decoder

⅛" stereo phone jack

Potentiometer

6-45

To protect the decoder and the other components, place them in a plastic job box.

To track bus

Decoder in project box

To speakers

6-46

I wired the decoder to the yard track bus and mounted the project box under the layout to complete the installation.

7-1

CHAPTER SEVEN

Running your railroad

A busy New Haven Alco RS-1 diesel road switcher shoves a string of cars down the yard lead past Bank Street tower. Using your model railroad to simulate realistic operation is a great way to share the hobby with others.

Once you've finished one or more sections of your model railroad, it's time to enjoy running your trains. Sometimes after a long day at work, I find nothing more relaxing than heading to the basement with a cup of tea and watching the trains run slowly through my layout's New England autumn scenery. It's a great way to spend a half hour and unwind.

However, there are other times when I want to do something more inter-active with the layout, and that's where operation comes into the picture, **7-1**. Operation is basically the game of running your model railroad like the real thing. Whether it's some simple switching work or running tightly scheduled passenger trains, you can add as much or as little operation to your layout as you like. And once you start, it's easy to expand.

This chapter looks at some techniques for getting your rolling stock ready for operation and then covers some of the basic principles you'll need to start running trains realistically.

PROJECT 1: Making your freight cars prototypical

Moving freight is what pays the bills, so a railroad needs plenty of cars on hand to accommodate its customers. Even though the predominant car type on your layout may be something as plain as a 40-foot boxcar, it's still important to pay attention to the rolling stock you select. Having cars that fit the period and theme of your model railroad is a good first step, **7-2**, and making sure those cars run well is important too.

An amazing wealth of model freight cars is currently available in N, HO, and O scales. And while there's a good chance you'll be able to find the cars you want for your layout, having so many choices can cause pitfalls. By paying close attention to the models you purchase and using some simple weathering techniques, you can easily add good-running, good-looking rolling stock to your layout.

STEP 1 Choosing cars that fit

If you're modeling a specific era, you need models that fit your period. One way to check a model for era-appropriateness is to look for the car's built date. The built date on this New Haven insulated boxcar is 1953, **7-3**. Since I model 1959 and the paint scheme on the car is as it was delivered to the railroad, it fits my layout. If I were modeling 1949, it wouldn't be appropriate.

Be careful though, as built dates are not always a good indicator; this Spokane, Portland & Seattle (SP&S) car has a built date of 1946. So far, so good. But the car has reporting marks on it for the Burlington Northern, **7-4**. This means the model is decorated for an SP&S car after that railroad was merged into the BN in 1970, so it won't work.

Choosing cars that fit your railroad's theme is also something to keep in mind. I have one SP&S boxcar on my New England-themed layout already, which is fine. But the chances of there being a lot of cars from this Pacific Northwest

7-2

Although a model railroad can include a wide range of cars, it is important to select rolling stock that fits the period and theme of the railroad you are modeling.

7-3

Built date

With a built date of June 1953 and original prototype paint scheme, this New Haven insulated boxcar fits the Naugatuck Valley RR's 1959 time frame.

7-4

Restenciled reporting mark for BN

This car has a Burlington Northern reporting mark, so it is modeled on an SP&S car that was used after the SP&S merged into the BN in 1970, outside the period of the layout.

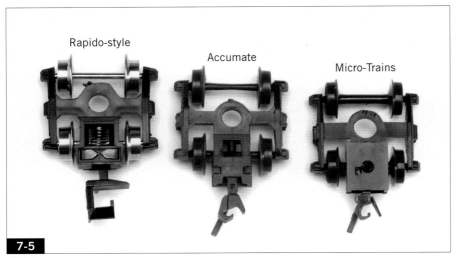

Although the Rapido-style coupler was once the standard for N scale models, modern Accumate and Micro-Trains couplers have a more realistic look.

7-6

Plastic wheelsets by Micro-Trains and Atlas and InterMountain metal wheelsets have a shallower flange than traditional ones for smoother running on code 55 rail.

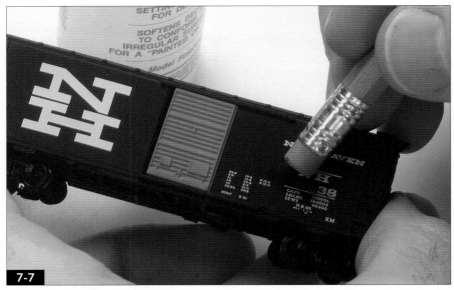

7-7

To remove an old car number, brush on some Micro-Sol and then rub off the softened ink with a standard no. 2 pencil eraser.

carrier running in Connecticut is slim. So unless there's a good reason for it, such as an industry that receives material from the Northwest, I shouldn't have too many SP&S cars in my fleet.

STEP 2 Choosing couplers and wheelsets

You have several choices when it comes to couplers for N scale models, **7-5**. (Modelers in HO have more choices.) For years, the Rapido-style coupler was the model railroad industry's standard N scale coupler. It worked reliably but didn't look anything like a prototype coupler.

Today, most modelers in N scale use some form of knuckle coupler, and the two most common choices are Accumate (made by Accurail and used on some car models such as Atlas) and Micro-Trains. While these two brands of couplers work fairly well together, you get the best results when using the same type of couplers, especially if you use magnetic uncoupling ramps.

Micro-Trains offers the widest variety of N scale coupler conversion kits for other manufacturers' models, and you can download a complete list at www.micro-trains.com.

Wheelsets are another important consideration, especially if you're using low-profile rail such as code 55 or smaller. Traditional wheelsets (often called pizza cutters because of their resemblance to the kitchen utensil) have extra-deep flanges. Besides looking less realistic, deeper-flanged wheelsets may bump the spike heads on some brands of track that use code 55 rail and will not run well.

Newer wheelsets have a much shallower flange including those manufactured by Micro-Trains, Atlas, and InterMountain, **7-6**. Most of these wheelsets snap into a model's existing trucks, so you can use them to replace pizza cutters or to outfit your cars with matching wheels.

STEP 3 Numbering individual cars

If you intend to operate your model railroad like the real thing, each car in your fleet needs a unique road number. Though some manufacturers provide sets of cars with individual numbers, most of the time you'll need to renumber some cars yourself.

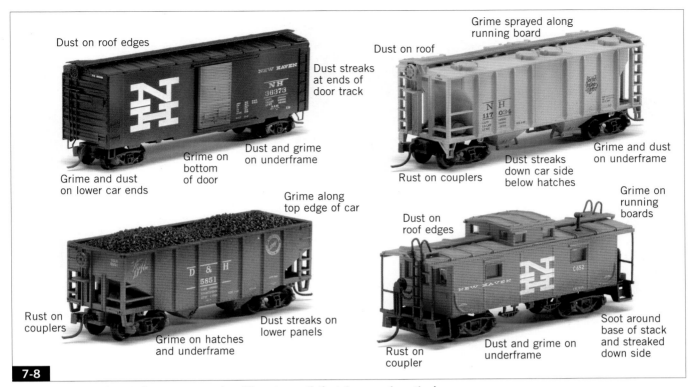

Dust on roof edges

Dust streaks at ends of door track

Grime on bottom of door

Dust and grime on underframe

Grime and dust on lower car ends

NEW HAVEN
NH 36979

Grime sprayed along running board

Dust on roof

Grime and dust on underframe

Dust streaks down car side below hatches

Rust on couplers

NH 117 034

Grime along top edge of car

Rust on couplers

Grime on hatches and underframe

Dust streaks on lower panels

D & H 5851

Grime on running boards

Dust on roof edges

Soot around base of stack and streaked down side

Dust and grime on underframe

Rust on coupler

NEW HAVEN
NH C652

7-8

Using the same basic techniques, you can give different cars distinct degrees of weathering.

To renumber a car, first remove part or all of the old number. One method I use is soaking the number with a little Microscale Micro-Sol, a decal solvent. Carefully brush the Micro-Sol on the printed numbers and then remove the softened ink with a pencil eraser, **7-7**. You'll need to repeat the process several times to completely remove the number. Be patient. Working too quickly can damage the car's paint or remove other printed details.

When the car's numbers are gone, I use decals to add new ones. If you're replacing only part of the car number, you'll need to find decals that match the existing lettering. I found that Microscale set no. MC-4354 for HO scale steam locomotives was a good match for the N scale boxcar shown in photo **7-7**.

STEP 4 Applying quick weathering

A little weathering goes a long way to remove the toy-like quality of brand new freight car models. You could use a number of different materials for this task, but I prefer to use an airbrush. Before spraying the cars, I remove the wheelsets and paint them separately.

I use three basic Polly Scale colors for weathering most of my freight cars:

L&N Gray for dust, Engine Black for road grime and soot, and Roof Brown for dark rust. I thin the paints 40 percent with rubbing alcohol and use a fine airbrush tip for spraying the models. This technique works well on both N and HO scales.

By the late 1950s, the New Haven was rather strapped for cash, so keeping the freight car fleet freshly painted was considered a luxury. Since the New Haven's freight cars were pretty dirty most of the time, I wanted mine to look that way too, **7-8**.

To weather a car, I usually start by spraying a dust coat of L&N Gray on the running gear, ends, and roof edges and use it to make streaks on the carbody. I then apply thinned Engine Black to the underside of the car and any place that needs extra grime. I reserve the rust for truck springs, couplers, and some of the brake rigging. It's a good idea to vary the weathering on your freight cars, so some look newer than others.

STEP 5 Dulling coupler pins

With the weathering work complete, I snap the wheelsets back in the trucks and then perform one last task before

sending the cars to the layout. Some cars, particularly Micro-Trains models, have shiny metal coupler pins. These stand out like sore thumbs, especially in photographs. To dull them, I brush-paint the pins with Polly Scale UP Dark Gray, **7-9**. Avoid getting paint on the moving parts of the couplers as it will gum up the works and keep them from working properly.

When the coupler pins have dried, I test the couplers to make sure they still work. I then move on to project 2, filling out car cards for the new cars. With that, the cars are ready to place into service on the layout, so they can begin earning their keep.

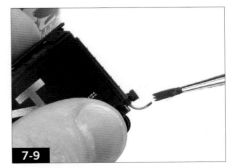

7-9

Brushing Polly Scale UP Dark Gray on shiny metal coupler pins gives them a dull, weathered finish.

Using a car-card-and-waybill system gives model railroaders an interactive and realistic way to move freight cars around the layout.

PROJECT 2:
Moving freight and making names

Once you've run a few trains on your layout, you may find yourself asking, "Is this all there is?" Though part of the allure of model railroading is watching your trains travel through towns and scenic landscapes, this limited level of participation gets old quickly. However, if you find yourself occasionally stopping a train to switch out a car or two at an industry, you're ready to start one of the more enjoyable aspects of the hobby – operation.

The motive behind the construction and operation of all prototype railroads is to make money, a purpose directly linked to the trains a railroad runs and how it conducts its day-to-day business. Though most model railroads don't actually turn a profit, adopting the idea of operating trains with a purpose will make your layout more interactive and realistic.

There are many ways to add prototype operating practices to your model railroad, and it's best to get started with something basic, such as freight car routing, **7-10**.

STEP 1 Mapping your railroad

Whether you're modeling a stretch of real railroad or freelancing your own line, you'll need to know how it fits into the outside world before you can start moving freight. Making your own system map is the first step, **7-11**. All you need is a railroad atlas or a detailed road map that shows railroad grades.

For my layout, set along the Naugatuck River Valley in Connecticut, I used a highlighter to mark the location of the main line and its north and east branches on my atlas, **7-12**. This step is especially important if you haven't modeled a specific place because it will give a frame of reference for your railroad's connections with other lines.

Next, pick names for your towns. If you're modeling real places with landmarks that people will recognize, go ahead and use the actual town names. However, if your locations aren't that specific, you may want to consider creating new towns on your map. For example, there are four towns on my layout, the focal point being Waterbury. Because it's the key to my entire railroad, I've modeled certain city features faithfully enough to look like Waterbury. The other three towns, however, are generic New England communities.

A system map shows you how your railroad fits into its surroundings and is the first step in moving freight. *Bill Zuback*

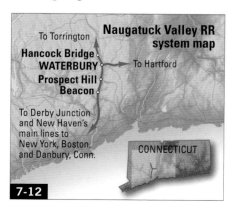

Illustration by Rick Johnson

On-line Industry List				
Town	Beacon			
Industry	Inbound/outbound	Car type	Material	Frequency
Hanson Piano Co.	inbound	boxcar	hardwoods	1/week
	inbound	boxcar	frame castings	1 every other week
	inbound	boxcar	wire	1 every other week
	inbound	boxcar	crating lumber	1/week
	outbound	boxcar	pianos	1-2/week
	outbound	gondola	scrap wood	1 every other week (gon stays until filled)
Connecticut Trim Co.	inbound	boxcar	hardwoods	1 every other week
	inbound	boxcar	softwoods	1/week
	outbound	boxcar	milled trim and moldings	1-2/week
	outbound	boxcar	sawdust	1/week (car stays until filled)
Johnson Textiles	inbound	boxcar	raw wool or cotton	1-2/week
	inbound	tank car	dyes and chemicals	1 every other week
	inbound	boxcar	cardboard shipping cartons	1-2/week
	outbound	boxcar	cloth	1-4/week

7-13

An industry list helps analyze the shipping and receiving requirements for each industry on your layout. This list is for my town of Beacon.

FORM 146-S

Switch list

TRAIN **23** COND. _____ DATE **Oct 7 1959** TIME **A.M.**

No.	Car Initials	Car Number	Car Type	Destination	Remarks
1	NH	35143	X	B/Hanson P.	
2	CP	100197	X	B/Conn. Trim	
3	NH	31728	X	B/Johnson Text	
4	BREX	75280	R	PH/Jandt Cold St	
5	D&H	5792	H	PH/Grivno Coal	
6	NH	61021	G	HB/JDH Metals	
7					
8					
9					
10					

7-14

A switch list, with columns for car initials, car number, car type, and destination, can be made on a computer with word processing software.

7-15

Go down a switch list town by town and select car models that meet each industry's needs to make up a train. *Bill Zuback*

I could have named these for real places on the Naugatuck line too, but instead, I made up names for the other towns (which I think is a lot more fun), basing them on features of the Naugatuck Valley. For instance, following a New England practice of using the same name over in a given region, I set my town of Beacon between the town of Beacon Falls and Beacon Hill Creek.

STEP 2 Performing an industry analysis

The second step is to perform an industry analysis of your layout and determine the products your on-line customers make, the materials they use, and how often they receive supplies or ship finished goods. By making a chart, you can figure out the shipping and receiving requirements for each industry on your layout, **7-13**.

Many industries are self-explanatory, such as a coal dealer – loads come in, and empties go out. All you'll need to do is determine the frequency. Others, however, take some research for modeling delivery and shipping cycles.

For the car requirements of more complex industries, let common sense be your guide to get up and running quickly. Later, when you've had time to complete some research, you can update your analysis to match the prototype.

One other important consideration is that most industries don't use all the material they receive, so don't forget to include carloads of waste products on your list. The piano factory on my layout ships out carloads of scrap wood and sawdust from time to time.

STEP 3 Starting with switch lists

Now that you know the location and requirements of your industries, your railroad can start serving them. A method that works particularly well with small railroads is a switch list.

7-16

When a car is assigned a load, it is given a waybill that is attached to its car card. Here, this reefer is being routed through Bridgeport with a load of potatoes. *Bill Zuback*

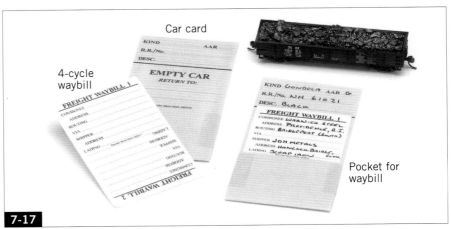

Car card

4-cycle waybill

Pocket for waybill

7-17

With a four-cycle waybill, a car is routed to four different locations, on or off the layout. *Bill Zuback*

107

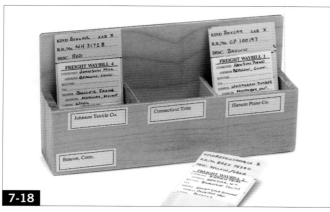

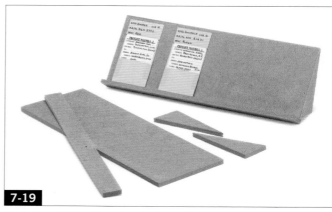

| 7-18 | 7-19 |

On a card box, you can label each slot with the industry's name and also list the town's name. *Bill Zuback*

Made from ¼" hardboard, a shelf provides a place for train crews to sort their car cards. *Bill Zuback*

A switch list is a nearly universal form used by railroaders to plan and record car movements. Though some are more elaborate than others, all have the same basic information, including spaces for car identification and destination. I made mine on my computer using Microsoft Word, **7-14**.

To make up a train using a switch list, start by looking at your industry analysis sheet to determine which businesses will receive cars this trip. Proceed down the list town by town, selecting car models to meet each industry's requirements, filling out the switch list as you go, **7-15**.

There are several ways to handle cars waiting to be picked up at industries. The easiest is to walk around to each industry on the layout and add those cars to your switch list, marking a P for pickup in the remarks column. When you've finished the list, assemble the train and give the list to the crew.

As you get into the habit of using switch lists, you'll find you can take shortcuts, such as using abbreviations for town and industry names.

STEP 4 Using car cards and waybills

Working with switch lists is fun, but filling out the paperwork for every train can get tedious. Car cards and waybills offer an interesting, flexible solution, and after filling out the forms once, the system can run itself forever.

With a car-card-and-waybill system, every freight car on the layout gets its own card that lists its reporting marks and type, as well as what to do

with the car when it's empty. When the car is assigned a load, it's then given a waybill, which is attached to the car card, **7-16**. The waybill lists the destination, lading, and routing information for the car. Since the car card follows its car around the layout, a train crew can look at the waybill at any given time to see how they should handle the car.

Several manufacturers offer car cards, or you can buy computer software to make your own. For my layout, I used the car routing system (no. 82916) from Micro-Mark. (This same set is also offered by Doc's Caboose.) It comes with paper car cards and special, four-cycle waybills, **7-17**.

A four-cycle waybill actually has four waybills printed on it, each with a number. When filled out and assigned to a freight car, that car is then routed to four different locations on or off the layout. (Off-layout destinations are represented by storage tracks called staging yards.) After the car arrives at a destination, the waybill is cycled (flipped over), revealing a new destination for the car. The process is repeated until the car ends up at its starting point, where you can either send it through the cycle again or swap its waybill with a different one. This way, your train crews don't see the same car showing up in the same place session after session.

Micro-Mark's car routing set is very easy to use and comes with a short instruction book to help you fill out the paperwork and get things rolling. You can also use switch lists with the car card system to help crews keep track of

their work, though the four-cycle waybills now determine movements.

STEP 5 Adding boxes and shelves

When you drop off a car at an industry, you'll need a place to put its car card and waybill. That's where bill boxes come in handy. Though I've made my own in the past, the waybill kit from Micro-Mark includes some nice, three-slot card boxes. You'll need one compartment for each industry on your layout. You can make computer-generated labels for the boxes, cementing them in place with a glue stick, to organize the boxes, **7-18**.

Train crews have a tendency to sort their car cards on layout surfaces. To solve this problem, you can make sorting shelves. Mine are made from ¼" hardboard and joined together with carpenter's glue, **7-19**. The overall size is 4" x 12". Once the glue dries, fasten the shelves to the layout next to your bill boxes. I placed one at each town and two at the yard in Waterbury.

PROJECT 3: Using sequence operation

Now that you've got a system to move freight over your railroad, let's look at how to get it there on time. Following is an account of how I designed the operating schematic for my layout, basing it upon the prototype traffic patterns of the New Haven RR. Also included is a synopsis of a typical operating session to give you an idea of how the sequence all fits together.

Even if you haven't modeled your railroad after a specific prototype, sequence operation is easy to add to most any layout: simply determine a schedule for your trains and then run them in that order, **7-20**. After you've finished the sequence, you can start your next operating session back at step one. Let's start by examining how the New Haven ran the line in the 1950s.

Modeling the Naugatuck

I chose to model the New Haven's Naugatuck line in the 1950s because I thought it would be a great fit for a mid-size operating model railroad. In the later '50s, the city of Waterbury saw two inbound and two outbound daily freight trains, an assortment of small way freights, and 10 daily commuter trains. Waterbury also had an impressive depot, a yard with local switching crews, an active freight house, and an operating interlocking tower (S.S. 202) at Bank Street Junction. The tower operator was also the dispatcher for the rest of the Naugatuck Branch.

During this time, Waterbury received a daily freight from Cedar Hill Yard (New Haven) and one from Maybrook Yard in New York. These trains would terminate in Waterbury's yard where their cars were classified for the area's way freights, Waterbury's freight house, and local switching.

All the way freights were run as turns, originating in Waterbury and returning at the end of the work day. The north train (NX16) switched industries from Waterbury to Winsted. Another train (NX15) worked the line south from Waterbury to Naugatuck. The third train (NX17) switched the Highland Branch that ran between Waterbury and Hartford. Waterbury's yard crew switched the city's local industries as well as those along the Watertown branch. When the way freights returned, the yard crew made up the trains that returned cars south to Cedar Hill and Maybrook.

Late 1950s passenger traffic on the Naugatuck was mostly handled by Budd Rail Diesel Cars (RDCs). There were four daily commuter trains each

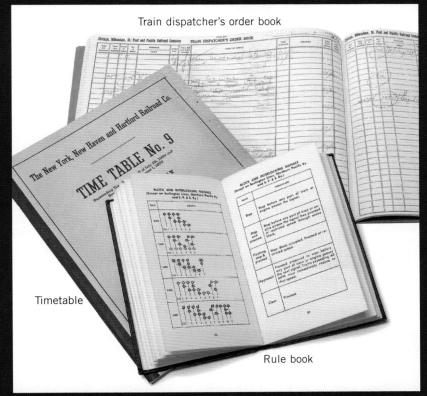

Information sources for operation

Train dispatcher's order book

Timetable

Rule book

Bill Zuback

There are many different resources you can consult about operation. Here are a few suggested starting points. I've used them all and have found them very helpful.

- Tony Koester's book *Realistic Model Railroad Operation* offers a detailed look at model railroad operation. It includes a great quick-start guide to get beginners up and running.

- *Starting Operation* is a downloadable PDF file from Information Station at www.modelrailroader.com. It includes 40 pages of articles from *Model Railroader* magazine covering a host of different operating ideas.

- Railroad rule books are often available at train shows or on Internet sites such as eBay. Though the rule book will provide more information than you'll need to run your layout, you'll learn a lot about how the prototype did things.

- An employee timetable, like a rule book, is another helpful prototype source. If you can get one for the railroad and era you're modeling, you'll find out all sorts of things about the trains your railroad ran.

- Train dispatcher's order books and other prototype operating paperwork such as train orders, switch lists, and clearance cards are useful items if you can find them. These provide real examples of how a railroad conducted its day-to-day activities.

7-20

A morning commuter train loads passengers in front of Waterbury's depot. The commuter trains, as well as the rest of the Naugatuck Valley RR, run following a set sequence of events that make up one 24-hour operating day.

Operating sequence on the Naugatuck

1. ND-2, Cedar Hill/Waterbury freight arrives in Waterbury Yard

2. Morning yard crew called

3. Maybrook/Waterbury freight arrives in Waterbury yard

4. Train 460, Waterbury/Hartford RDC departs

5. Train 451, Waterbury/Bridgeport RDCs leave Waterbury

6. NX15 departs Waterbury, works line south to Beacon and returns

7. Train 452, Bridgeport/Waterbury RDCs return/depart as Train 453

8. *River Job* called

9. NX17 departs, swaps cars in staging, and waits for return time

10. Train 454, Bridgeport/Waterbury

11. NX16 leaves Waterbury, switches Hancock Bridge, and waits for return time

12. Train 455, Waterbury/Bridgeport

13. Afternoon yard crew called

14. Hartford/Maybrook train stops in Waterbury to drop transfer cars

15. NX17 returns to Waterbury

16. Train 456, Bridgeport/Waterbury

17. NX16 returns to Waterbury

18. Train 461, Hartford RDC returns

19. Train 457, Waterbury/Bridgeport

20. Night Maybrook freight departs

21. Train 458, last Bridgeport RDC

22. DN-1, Cedar Hill freight departs

way from Waterbury to Bridgeport. This was pretty much the same train, made up of two or three RDCs, and it ran back and forth all day (about an hour each way). At Bridgeport, passengers could board trains west to New York or east to New Haven and on to Boston. There was also a daily commuter run from Waterbury east along the Highland Branch to Hartford. This train left Waterbury in the morning for Hartford and returned in the late afternoon. The RDCs were stored at Waterbury overnight, and there was typically a spare car on hand in case of extra traffic or a mechanical failure.

Operating on the layout

The design for my Naugatuck Valley RR leans heavily toward operation. The layout centers on Waterbury and includes as many of the New Haven's connecting lines and operating characteristics as possible. The Waterbury portion features key elements such as Bank Street Junction, **7-21**, the depot, **7-20**, the lower yard, and the freight house, **7-24**, although all had to be compressed to fit. Beyond that, the towns and industries on the rest of the railroad are freelanced; I chose good operating characteristics over attempting to re-create the prototype. The final combination still says "New Haven" but fits a model railroad format.

Though the layout takes up the space of a spare bedroom, don't be fooled by its small size. The industrial switching work, yard and freight house operations, and moderate schedule of commuter trains will keep a crew of six operators busy for an entire evening. Running trains at prototypical speeds also helps make the railroad seem bigger than it really is.

A typical operating session requires a yardmaster, four road engineers, and a dispatcher. The commuter RDCs are run by anyone available at the moment, including the dispatcher. The railroad is set up for sequence operation (running trains following a set order). I like the sequence method because I can run a session by myself over the course of several evenings, one job at a time – something that occurs more frequently than getting a group together.

Running a typical session

The sequence for a typical operating day is shown on the opposite page. The first jobs called are the morning Waterbury yard crew and crews for the Cedar Hill and Maybrook trains. Once the two freight trains arrive in Waterbury, the yard crew sorts the cars for the three turns and for the local switch run. While that happens, the RDCs make their initial trips of the day to Bridgeport and Hartford. The Hartford RDC runs into staging and stays there until it returns in the afternoon. The Bridgeport train makes stops at all the stations on its way south.

The first way freight out of the yard is NX15. This train works the towns south of Waterbury, **7-22**. The tire plant and the A&P warehouse at Prospect Hill provide switching work. Also, the busy RDC traffic between Waterbury and Bridgeport keeps the crew members of NX15 on their toes since they need to keep the station tracks clear for the commuter trains.

The Hartford way freight (NX17) is out of the yard next. This train runs into staging, swaps cars with a cut in storage, and then returns to Waterbury later in the session. The Hartford cars left in staging at the end of the session are rotated off the layout and replaced by different cars from the pool.

Once the Hartford train is set for its return trip, the same crew then takes NX16 north to Winsted. Currently, the north part of the line on the layout runs only as far as Hancock Bridge. This is a narrow little town along the back wall of the basement. I was originally going to make it just another staging yard, similar to the one used for Hartford, but I decided to include several small industry flats and a depot to make it more interesting. After the crew of NX16 finishes the switching work, like the Hartford run, it picks up another string of cars, this time from the Hancock Bridge siding, and readies its train to return to Waterbury later in the day, **7-23**.

While the yard crew is busy getting the turns out of the yard, the *River Job* crew starts its day. The first task is to switch cars at the freight house. Waterbury had a very active four-track freight house, **7-24**. The prototype saw

7-21

In addition to the brick station, another icon of New Haven railroading in Waterbury is Bank Street Junction. Here, the Naugatuck River line split from the Danbury line. Although the Danbury main had been abandoned before the 1950s, the Bank Street tower was still in service, and its operator dispatched the Naugatuck Branch.

7-22

Train NX15 crosses the Naugatuck River south of Waterbury on its way to switch the towns of Prospect Hill and Beacon. This train is one of three turns that switch the Naugatuck and its connecting branch lines.

7-23

NX16 runs up the north branch through Hancock Bridge. Once switching at the local industries is completed, the train will return to Waterbury. Completing the northern branch is the next Naugatuck Valley RR expansion project.

Waterbury's freight house saw a lot of traffic, making it an ideal industry to include on the layout. During a typical session, the freight house receives more cars than all of the other Waterbury industries combined.

The crew of the *River Job* uses an Alco RS-1 to pull empty hoppers from Grivno Coal. Once the cars are clear of the facing-point turnout, the crew will shove them through the switchback and then pull them uphill to return to the main line and swap them for inbound cars.

Near the end of the operating session, *Model Railroader* columnist Mike Polsgrove works the Waterbury yard, sorting cars for the evening outbound trains to the New Haven's yards at Cedar Hill, Conn., and Maybrook, N.Y.

more cars through it on an average day than my staging area and yard tracks can supply for the entire model railroad during an operating session, so I cut the structure down to fit. I built it to serve just two tracks, and the model is about half the prototype's actual length. Near the freight house, I also added a car clean-out track. This provides extra switching work as cars are periodically dropped here to have their interiors cleaned before being used again.

After switching the freight house and cleaning track, the *River Job* crew next picks up cars for the industries nestled along the Naugatuck River on the south side of the city, **7-25**. Though there are currently just three of them, switching these industries is somewhat of a puzzle. To get down to river level, the train must use a switchback, the tail of which is big enough for only a locomotive and four 40-foot cars. There is no runaround track here, and two of the three industries have facing-point switches, so all runaround moves must be made on the main line.

The key to success on the *River Job* is to pull all the outbound cars first. With that done, you can bring in the inbound facing-point cars, and things are fairly straightforward after that.

For more operation, I've included a Hartford/Maybrook train on the schedule. It was discontinued on the real railroad in 1954. I've also added a Waterbury stop, so it can drop off a few Hartford transfer cars before heading south (and back to the staging yard).

By this point in the session, the afternoon yard crew is on duty, sorting cars from the arriving turns to put together the Cedar Hill and Maybrook trains, **7-26**. These outbound trains depart in the early evening hours. Also, the RDCs make their final runs and then tie up for the night at the depot.

With that, a session on the Naugatuck is finished. Preparing for the next session is fairly easy. I use car cards with four-cycle waybills, so I turn the waybills to the next step for all but in-transit cars and start again.

Sharing your model railroad with others by hosting operating sessions is all part of the fun of building a layout. I wish you all the best in your endeavors!